The Introvert's Way

LIVING A

QUIET LIFE

IN A

NOISY WORLD

Sophia Dembling

Ms. Elsie Bendiksen
1 Blossom St.
Fairhaven, MA 02719

The Introvert's Way

"Sophia Dembling is proof of the vitality under the still surface of introversion. Her voice is candid, witty, and refreshing, exposing the often inane myths we swallow whole when we use extroversion as our standard of health. *The Introvert's Way* is an enjoyable and liberating read."

—Laurie Helgoe, PhD, author of *Introvert Power:
Why Your Inner Life Is Your Hidden Strength*

"For the 70 percent of highly sensitive people who are introverts, *The Introvert's Way* will give them practical ideas for dealing with others and for feeling fine about themselves, just as they are—loving quiet, solitude, and deep conversation."

—Elaine N. Aron, PhD, author of *The Highly Sensitive Person*

"With a mix of real-life examples, empirical research, and a big dose of humor, Dembling's book is a call to arms for introverts to self-identify and accept their uniqueness."

—Irene S. Levine, PhD, Professor of Psychiatry,
NYU School of Medicine

"Author Sophia Dembling's unique voice brilliantly captures and validates the introvert experience. She explodes myths and weaves in research and suggestions with laugh-out-loud writing. Whether an introvert or extrovert, the chapter titles alone will make you smile."

—Jennifer B. Kahnweiler, PhD, author of
The Introverted Leader: Building on Your Quiet Strength

"Our society is in the midst of a quiet but powerful revolution that is finally acknowledging the experiences and strengths of introverts. I celebrate Sophia's book as a welcome addition to the growing body of literature on the subject. Her honesty, humor, and approachability make the quiet life appealing!"

—Adam S. McHugh, author of *Introverts in the Church:
Finding Our Place in an Extroverted Culture*

The Introvert's Way

Living a Quiet Life
in a Noisy World

Sophia Dembling

A PERIGEE BOOK

A PERIGEE BOOK
Published by the Penguin Group
Penguin Group (USA) Inc.
375 Hudson Street, New York, New York 10014, USA

Penguin Group (Canada), 90 Eglinton Avenue East, Suite 700, Toronto, Ontario M4P 2Y3, Canada (a division of Pearson Penguin Canada Inc.) • Penguin Books Ltd., 80 Strand, London WC2R 0RL, England • Penguin Group Ireland, 25 St. Stephen's Green, Dublin 2, Ireland (a division of Penguin Books Ltd.) • Penguin Group (Australia), 250 Camberwell Road, Camberwell, Victoria 3124, Australia (a division of Pearson Australia Group Pty. Ltd.) • Penguin Books India Pvt. Ltd., 11 Community Centre, Panchsheel Park, New Delhi—110 017, India • Penguin Group (NZ), 67 Apollo Drive, Rosedale, Auckland 0632, New Zealand (a division of Pearson New Zealand Ltd.) • Penguin Books (South Africa) (Pty.) Ltd., 24 Sturdee Avenue, Rosebank, Johannesburg 2196, South Africa

Penguin Books Ltd., Registered Offices: 80 Strand, London WC2R 0RL, England

While the author has made every effort to provide accurate telephone numbers, Internet addresses, and other contact information at the time of publication, neither the publisher nor the author assumes any responsibility for errors, or for changes that occur after publication. Further, the publisher does not have any control over and does not assume any responsibility for author or third-party websites or their content.

First edition: December 2012

Library of Congress Cataloging-in-Publication Data

Dembling, Sophia.
The introvert's way : living a quiet life in a noisy world / Sophia Dembling. —1st ed.
p.   cm. — (A Perigee book)
Includes index.
ISBN 978-0-399-53769-1
1. Introversion.   2. Introverts.   3. Interpersonal relations.   I. Title.
BF698.35.I59D46   2012
155.2'32—dc23   2012029244

PRINTED IN THE UNITED STATES OF AMERICA

10 9 8 7 6 5 4 3 2 1

Most Perigee books are available at special quantity discounts for bulk purchases for sales promotions, premiums, fund-raising, or educational use. Special books, or book excerpts, can also be created to fit specific needs. For details, write: Special Markets, Penguin Group (USA) Inc., 375 Hudson Street, New York, New York 10014.

ALWAYS LEARNING   PEARSON

Dedicated to Tom because I love him
and because he gets me.

Contents

Introverts Unite   1

What Would Jung Say?   5

The Great American Racket   10

Science Says We're Not Necessarily Shy   14

Born to Be Mild   18

Quiet Riot   22

Just Intense Enough   25

The Slow Train of Thought   29

The Internal Flame   32

What Quiet Says   35

The Fertile Void   39

I Like to Watch   44

Energy In, Energy Out   48

"We Didn't Know You Were an Introvert,
      We Thought You Were Just a Bitch."   52

Magic Words to Plug Energy Drains   55

Introverts Are Not Failed Extroverts   58

I Like People, Just Not All People All the Time   62

Don't Call Us, We'll Call . . . Well, No,
     Maybe We Won't   65

We Gotta Fight for Our Right Not to Party   70

Loneliness Is a State of Mind   74

The Happiness Bias   77

Who's a Narcissist?   82

Turning the Extrovert Advantage Upside Down   86

The Party Predicament   90

The Bathroom and Other Party Survival Skills   93

Hell Is a Cocktail Party   96

Fact 1: Some People Are Boring.
     Fact 2: You Are Not Obligated to Listen
     to Them.   100

Saying Yes When You Want to
     Say No (and Vice Versa)   104

Extroversion in a Bottle   109

There Must Be Fifty Ways to Leave a Party   113

Life Through Introvert Eyes   116

"It'll Be Fun!" They Say, But We Beg to Differ   119

Fun, Introvert Style   123

Friends, "Friends," Acquaintances,
     and Why Bother?   126

The Online Extrovert   130

The Happy Noise of Extroversion   135

Because They Love You 139

Itty-Bitty Introverts 143

Love Us, but Leave Us Alone (Sometimes) 148

I F#&$ing Hate It When They Say That 154

A Team of One 157

Introvert Feats of Derring-Do 162

First, Leave the House and Other Tips
for Making Friends 164

Mind Fullness to Mindfulness 168

Mistakes Introverts Make 172

Affirmations for Introverts 176

Middle Ground 180

C'mon People Now, Smile on Your Brother 183

ACKNOWLEDGMENTS 187

INDEX 189

Introverts Unite

have to admit, there were times over the course of my life—and I've been around a few decades—when even I wondered if maybe I were some kind of coldhearted snob. Why was I so reluctant to go to parties and why did I want to leave them shortly after arriving? Why did I get annoyed if a date with a friend turned into a group outing? Why was I so picky, picky, picky about who I spent time with? Why did weekly check-in phone calls from friends get on my nerves? Why did gregarious people cause me to back away slowly? Why did I like being alone so much?

Was I shy? Mean? Judgmental? Misanthropic? Dour? Did I hate people? Was I socially stunted? What was wrong with me, and how could I change and be the kind of backslapping, fun-for-all type of person that everyone seems to prefer?

Why?

Because that's not my nature.

I am an introvert. And there's not a damn thing wrong with me.

I started learning about introversion a couple of years ago, and it's completely changed my perception of myself—for the better. I don't hate people. I'm not unfriendly or stuck-up. I'm not shy, socially awkward, or in any way (that I know of) socially inept. I am perfectly capable of carrying on a conversation. I can even speak in public and do so fairly often. To meet me, you might think I'm extroverted. I'm not, but a lot of people don't understand introversion.

When I identify myself as an introvert, some people try to argue with me. They say I can't be an introvert because I am capable of leaving the house, of being social, of making conversation.

They don't get it.

The difference between extroverts and introverts is not that the former are good at socializing and the latter aren't. Or that introverts dislike people and extroverts never met a stranger. Or that introverts don't like to talk and extroverts love a nice, long chat. Or that introverts prefer books and extroverts prefer sports.

In a way, it's all of those things. And in a way, it's none.

One thing is sure, though: The more I understand introversion, the more comfortable I am with it, and with myself. So I thought I'd share. The goal of this book is to spread the good word about living as an introvert and to help you find the same quiet comfort with yourself as I have.

My first essay about introversion was called "Confessions of an Introverted Traveler" and it was published on a website called *World Hum*. The response was immediate and enormous. Thousands of views, hundreds of comments, gallons of gratitude, and countless people echoing "hell yeah!" When I started blogging about introversion in 2009, and started comparing notes with thousands of introverts who responded to the blog, I found that underneath all our American chatter is a subculture of people who speak only when we have something to say, who like people but don't need a thousand friends, and who can enjoy parties sometimes, but in our own way.

All our lives, we introverts have bought into the myth that extroversion is better and is the American way. In a nation that holds extroversion in the highest esteem, introverts get pressure every which way to behave differently. Conventional wisdom insists that America is a nation of extroverts—of glad-handers and random smilers, of party on and the more the merrier. Introversion is considered odd, distressing, even serial killer–ish. Introverts are urged to get out there, work the room, join the team. Parents worry about children who would rather play alone in their rooms than join the gang in the playground. Bookish teenagers are exhorted to break out of their shells. Adults are chastised if they would rather work alone than as team players.

We have been told that too much solitude is unhealthy. That we're "too intense" because we prefer deep, thoughtful conversation to cheerful chitchat. We are sometimes considered snobbish because we don't think that two is necessarily better than one, and prefer one-on-one or small groups to large gatherings.

The things extroverts think are great fun—parties, group activities, chatting up strangers–aren't fun for us, which marks us as strange to many people. And sometimes well-meaning folks actually grab our arms and try to drag us into doing things we don't think are fun. The hokey-pokey. Sing-alongs. Bed-and-breakfasts. Sometimes we go to the theater and get stuck in that very special hell that is audience participation. We often attend parties out of a sense of obligation rather than with pleasure.

Having been told all our lives that our way is not the right way, we've spent our lives trying to "come out of our shell," or else bit our tongues and indulged our introversion surreptitiously, like it's a dirty secret. But the fact is, introverts are legion, and dying for affirmation.

That's where this book comes in.

Fellow introverts, it's time for us to stop pretending, it's time to stop apologizing for who we are. Just because we are capable of presenting an extroverted face to the world doesn't mean we are required to. It's up to us. Introversion is not wrong, extroversion is not right—and vice versa. We are who we are and that's what makes the world interesting.

In this book, I'll lay out both the problems and the solutions, what we are and what we aren't, what we could be and what we don't have to be if we don't want to. Introversion is not an illness, it's not a pathology, it's not a bad thing. It's simply a way of functioning in the world and there's not a darn thing wrong with it.

It's time we embrace our nature and start defending our case. Quietly.

What Would Jung Say?

S o, what exactly is introversion?

That depends on who you ask.

Sigmund Freud, in his Debbie Downer way, considered introversion pathological and a form of neurosis. He defined it as "the turning away of the libido from the possibilities of real satisfaction . . ." In other words, he believed people are introverted because they can't face reality and think they'll never have sex. Happily, this sex-obsessed Freudian spin doesn't drive the conversation anymore, although shades of it live on in the stereotype of the bathrobe-clad introvert virgin living in his mother's basement.

Since Freud's day, the definition of introversion has morphed and changed and grown, and it continues to. It turns out that introversion is actually kind of a slippery concept to pin down. The more we look at it, the more it shape-shifts. Researchers are still trying to hammer out a definition that is inclusive of all the nuances of introversion, while at the same time teasing apart the differences between introversion and shyness, and sensory sensitivity, and other things that come up when introverts describe introversion. And scientists would love to find a definition that can help them with empirical research in psychology and cognition labs.

C. G. Jung, a protégé of Freud who tired of all his mentor's sex talk and negativity, broke away to do his own thinking and put a less dreary spin on introversion and extroversion—words he is credited with popularizing, by the way. Jung was the first to propose the model of psychic energy, suggesting that for introverts, energy flows inward, while for extroverts, energy flows outward. Introverts tend to embrace this definition. It feels right for us because we know exactly what it feels like to have our energy depleted when we have sent too much flowing outward. A weekend of heavy socializing can put me in a coma for a couple of days after. A week of heavy socializing and I need to live in a cave for at least a week.

This energy-in/energy-out theory continues to drive general discussion, although defining "psychic energy" is all but impossible and measuring it in the lab is even harder. Still, it's one of those things most of us understand at practically a cellular level. Too bad "I just know" is not good enough for scientists to hang any sort of data on.

Hans Eysenck, a German-British psychologist, brought sociability into the discussion. Eysenck considered introversion the opposite of extroversion, which he described as being outgoing, sociable, enthusiastic, and impulsive. By this model, introverts sound like a pretty glum bunch to me; words that are the opposite of Eysenck's definition of extroversion include "unsociable," "unenthusiastic," "aloof." If Freud gave us the sad sack–virgin model of introversion, Eysenck may be held partially responsible for the antisocial misanthrope stereotype. (Although, if we review those extrovert traits, we can perhaps agree that impulsivity isn't necessarily something to be proud of. So score one for the introverts.) Eysenck was also the first to suggest that introversion and extroversion might be physiological; that the brains of extroverts crave more arousal than the brains of introverts.

Not that Eysenck is all wrong about introversion, or necessarily critical of it. We *are*, in fact, less sociable than extroverts. We're okay with that definition. We just want to see that acknowledged in its own right rather than as a lack. (More on that later.) And we like the idea that introversion might actually be hardwired in, because we're tired of people trying to change us—or of feeling like we should change ourselves. If this is our essential nature, then changing it is impossible.

Starting in the 1960s, other personality theorists developed what is called the Big Five factors of personality, which are personality traits found to remain relatively stable over a lifetime and are generally viewed as existing on a continuum. Extroversion and its inverse, introversion, are among those traits. (The others are Openness, Conscientiousness, Neuroticism, and Agreeableness.) Each of us falls in a different place on the continuum for the traits. In this model, extroversion has six facets: warmth, gregariousness, assertiveness, activity, excitement-seeking, and positive emotions. Once more, if we extrapolate from that the inverse of extroversion, it's not pretty: cold, taciturn, compliant, sedentary, dull, and grumpy. I reject every one of those descriptions except maybe sedentary, which I can be at times. Also grumpy, which I also can be, but usually when my energy has been depleted by too much socializing.

In recent years the debate over what introversion is has continued, but it's come a long way since Freud's surly assessment. Using all the new whiz-bang brain-scanning technology available, researchers are actually starting to identify differences in the brains of introverts and extroverts, and people are beginning to come around to thinking that introversion might not be such a terrible thing—in fact, it might even have some really good qualities. Psychoanalyst and author Marti Laney was one of the early voices in what some people call the "pro-introvert" movement, and she's added a number of other qualities into the discussion: Deep thinkers. Creative. Self-reflective. Flexible. Responsible.

This is great, but it also sends attempts to define introversion spinning in a whole other direction. So does psychologist Elaine Aron's concept of the "Highly Sensitive Person" (HSP for short), which also has been jumbled into the mix because many introverts who have read her books have recognized themselves in there. HSPs are easily overwhelmed by too much fuss and bother, are sensitive to other people's moods, hyperaware of what's going on around them. This is a sensory processing matter. I've been known to walk into a big, busy party and go practically catatonic. Whether this sensitivity to outside stimuli is an aspect of introversion or something else altogether adds yet another layer of confusion to our definition of introversion.

And then there's the problem of the long reign of shyness as a synonym for introversion. All these years that researchers and others have used "introversion" and "shyness" interchangeably definitely muddies the waters, especially in the lab. A lot of past research has been conducted with shyness standing in for introversion, so while the research is interesting and partly relevant, it also is partly irrelevant. Still, we'll be looking at it here because, well, it's what we have at the moment. We're making do.

Despite the confusion, what is becoming increasingly clear is that introversion is more than just the absence of extroversion. As introverts, we take up our own space in the world, even if the shape of it is not yet fully defined. We're a little bit Jung, a little bit Eysenck. Laney makes us feel good and we like to think we're creative and deep thinkers and all those good things, but there's no empirical data to confirm all that. And lots of us relate to Aron's HSP, though the jury's out on whether that's introversion or something else.

But the good news is that more than ever before (thank you, World Wide Web), introverts are gathering, talking to each other, comparing notes, and taking ownership of our nature. Scientists may be doing the work in the lab, but we're doing field research. We're part of the movement to define, delineate, and understand introversion, and we're getting closer every day to figuring it out.

The Great American Racket

America is a noisy culture. We bellow at each other every which way—politicians and pundits, movie stars and reality-show stars, billboards and televisions, and cell phones and text messages all clamor for our attention. Headlines scream equally about car bombs and celebrity divorces; blockbuster movies get ever louder and increasingly expensive and disengaged from reality.

In TV-land, executives talk about needing "noisy" shows to cut through the clutter of hundreds of channels, hundreds of shows. *Blam! Slam! Explosions! Gunfire! Zombies! When animals attack!* Quiet shows about quiet emotions often die with a whisper within weeks of launching.

We've even cranked up the volume on grief. I was startled and disturbed by the orgy of public garment rending we saw after Princess Diana died. She seemed like a perfectly nice lady, but why did the wailing have to be so public and overwrought? Did everybody in the world have some kind of private relationship with her that I had missed out on? When did simple sadness become an inadequate expression of grief?

Facebook, too, has brought grief out in public, whether in response to celebrity news, such as Michael Jackson's death, or to private losses, which we announce with tearstained Facebook pages inviting all our "friends" to share our sorrow. We keep nothing quiet, and the louder we get, the louder we get, clamoring to be heard over the ambient racket we have created.

Not only has volume been ratcheted up but expectations have, too. Quiet success—painting a picture, writing a poem, writing an algorithm—is all well and good, but if you haven't become famous doing it, then did it really matter? If a tree falls in the forest and it isn't mentioned on CNN, did it really happen?

America's volume is cranked up to eleven.

And so, in a way, the nation seems more extroverted than ever. It's full of squeaking wheels, demanding our attention. Politics are loud and bellicose, and the most vocal and rude pundits get the most attention, in that way that you can't ignore a shrieking car alarm. Our quiet thinkers, eggheads, poets, and philosophers don't have a chance of being heard above the racket. Introverts are being drowned out altogether.

On a one-on-one level, extrovert to introvert, introverts retreat. When confronted by a chatterbox, we will simply mentally withdraw, letting the words stream over and around us while we sit quietly inside our heads. At a big busy party, we will seek out a place to sit out the hubbub, happy when anyone pauses for a visit, but not jumping up and joining the conga line.

Yet, it's not so simple when it comes to the macro view. We are

cogs in the machine—often important ones—whose contribu-
tions are often overlooked or downplayed. When a movie is a hit,
we credit the stars, not the writers. The pinnacle of success for a
book these days is to be made into a movie; once a story makes
sound, it's validated. Reality-show stars earn many times more
than librarians. (Not that it's impossible for librarians to be extroverts.) What do you suppose the ratio is of world-famous classical
musicians to world-famous young women who can dance and
sort of sing and look good half-dressed? Extroverts love the spotlight and they know how to get it.

Which is not to say that there is no such thing as extroverted
writers or introverted actors. One of the most extroverted writers
I know does a lot of ghostwriting, which requires crawling into
someone else's brain and letting that person live in hers. This
sounds unbearable to me. There's really not enough room in my
brain for anyone else. And introverted movie stars like Julia Roberts tend to get famous when they're in extrovert mode—acting,
chatting it up on talk shows, making red-carpet appearances.
Then, as soon as they can do so without risking their careers,
movie star introverts retreat into a well-protected life, keeping
tight control on who sees them when and how. Johnny Depp is a
good example of this. When he's not on-screen, he lives mostly
out of the public eye.

In some ways, all this is fine. Introverts don't like all eyes on
us anyway. But it can also be frustrating, when we have something to say but don't want to yell.

How do we break through the racket?

I remember once reading an interview with Marlon Brando,
who described creating his character in *The Godfather*. Brando

said he'd noticed that powerful people spoke quietly, and Don Corleone's quiet calm and nearly inaudible speaking voice are key to the character. When Corleone speaks, you have to be quiet to hear him. What can we learn from Don Corleone (that doesn't involve killing people)? That quiet does have its own power, if we can harness it.

Introverts are finding their voices and though each one is quiet, put them all together and you have a much louder quiet. Rather than trying to outyell America, we need to keep firmly and consistently speaking our truths. We start with the people closest to us, saying what we need and who we are as often as necessary until it sinks in. We stop apologizing or slinking away when we want to leave the party. We push back, gently, when anyone tries to shame us for our nature. Sometimes you don't have to say something loud to be heard if you say it consistently. One introvert at a time, we will eventually make America hear us.

Science Says We're Not Necessarily Shy

ntroverts get mistaken for extroverts all the time because a lot of people think introversion is the same as shyness.

It's not.

Yes, both shyness and introversion relate to socializing, but shy people are scared of socializing. Introverts just aren't always interested in it. While there can be crossover, they're not mutually exclusive.

Louis A. Schmidt, a neuroscientist at McMaster University who studies shyness, gave me a whole new way to think of introversion and shyness. He defines introversion as a motivation—in this case, a weak desire to be with people. Extroverts have a yen for company a whole lot more than introverts do.

Shyness, on the other hand, he describes as a behavior. Shy people are inhibited, tense, and uncomfortable in social situations. And while introverts can be shy, so can extroverts.

Schmidt further explains, "When we look at the interaction

between shyness and introversion and treat those as two unre-
lated dimensions, it's as though each independent measure is adding unique variants to behavior." Translated to non-neuroscientist,
that means that someone who is introverted and shy behaves differently from someone who is introverted and not shy, who behaves differently from someone who is extroverted and shy, who
behaves differently from someone who is extroverted and not shy.

The unhappiest combination is extroverted and shy. Those
sad souls want to socialize, but fear it. They're the ones who turn
up at every party and cower in the corner, or stand terrified and
tongue-tied at networking events, or maybe even rely on liquor to
bring out the party animal in them. (Introverts might also try this,
especially when they're young and trying to fit in to a college
party crowd. But they usually grow out of it. More on that later.)

I am introverted and not shy. This means when I want to step
out from inside my own head, I can do so without much trouble.
But I don't always want to. For example, my job often requires
traveling and touring different areas with groups of people. Some
days, I am right in the middle of things, chattering and joking and
bringing my happy noise to the proceedings. Other days, I'm just
not interested, so I hang back, let others have the spotlight, and
enjoy my own company. Actually, this can happen hour to hour.
I'm not a morning person, so I have my first cup of coffee in my
hotel room, however revolting the in-room coffee is (and it's usually pretty revolting). By afternoon, I might be in the mood for a
little friendly fun and chatter, but by evening I'm usually ready
to shut it down again.

To a large extent, shyness can be overcome. Introversion cannot, and that's okay. Introverts who have embraced their nature

don't feel like they're missing out on anything. Besides, many of us can behave like extroverts when we want to. If extreme introversion lies on one end of the continuum and extreme extroversion on the other, many of us live somewhere between the two, and the closer an introvert is to the middle, the easier extroverted behavior is. In one online discussion, a guy described himself as a "swashbuckling introvert," for his ability to swing into a room and put on a show. Another woman called herself an "extroverted introvert." When I decide to put on the extrovert, I call it my dog and pony show.

When we want to, not-shy introverts can nut up to the task of being charming and witty. We can meet new people. We can start conversations and keep them rolling, and even draw shy people out, since we're good at not getting up in anyone's face and we're patient listeners. We know how to ease into conversation in a way that doesn't frighten shrinking violets.

In some ways, the not-shy introvert could be considered to have superior social skills to extroverts because we can accept attention without requiring it. If I find myself in a situation where conversation needs to be perked up, I can do the perking. Introverts' listening skills serve us well in keeping conversation going because we really hear what people say, and know what to ask or add.

At the same time, if someone comes along who clearly desires the spotlight, we're equally happy to cede the stage. I accept attention, sometimes I invite it, but I don't compete for it. I can't, really. I'm not loud enough, bold enough, or insistent enough. I can shut down my dog and pony show as easily as I can crank it up, and with no resentment at all—often with some relief. I'm just as happy to be in the audience while someone else takes center stage. Or, for that matter, just slip out the back door and let the show go on without me.

Introverts who are not shy are used to being told that they could not possibly be introverts. This can be irritating, but think of it as a teachable moment. Remember: We can do everything extroverts do, and do it well. The difference is that after a while, we lose interest.

Born to Be Mild

Because introversion is one of those traits that stays pretty steady throughout the life span, it's likely that there's something going on in our brains to make it so, although researchers haven't exactly pinpointed it yet. Likely it's a bunch of somethings.

One study finds that introverts' brains pay the same amount of attention to inanimate objects as they do to human faces, unlike extroverts' brains, which pay more attention to faces. Another finds that extroverts' brains are more sensitive to rewards than introverts'. This may explain why, as some introverts insist (somewhat misanthropically), extroverts seem needy. They love rewards and find sociability rewarding.

Psychologist Elaine Aron has made a cottage industry of understanding and interpreting what she calls the Highly Sensitive Person (HSP). A lot of introverts relate to Aron's description of the HSP. We are easily rattled by a lot of noise and fuss, highly attuned to the moods and emotions of other people, have rich inner lives, think deeply, and are slow to warm up to new situations. It's not clear yet if all introverts are HSPs, but it seems to factor into the complicated framework that is our current understanding of introversion.

Employing magnetic resonance imaging, which measures brain activity, Aron has actually seen brain activity that supports her hypothesis about the slow, deep thinking of HSPs. She found that the brains of HSPs respond differently from non-HSPs to subtle or more obvious changes in photographs. HSPs looked longer at photos with subtle changes, and when they did, a whole bunch of brain areas lit up along with the visual areas, indicating that they were processing the images deeply.

So, with all this deep processing going on with something like a photograph, we can extrapolate that the real walking, talking, laughing, dancing, arguing, partying world keeps HSPs' busy brains on overdrive. And if this sensitivity is, in fact, a facet of introversion, Aron's research tells us that introverts' brains stay very busy all by themselves and are easily overwhelmed by too much going on around us. While the fuel that runs extroverts' brains is stimulation coming in, our brains generate their own heat. Too much outer stimulation and we blow a fuse.

That's probably why walking into a big, robust party can paralyze me (and other introverts). I struggle to focus my eyes, forget people's names, fight to form sentences. My brain simply can't process the scene, greet my hosts, and decide what I want to drink all at the same time. It's too much. My ears are ringing just writing this.

Other research indicates that the brains of extroverts require copious amounts of the neurotransmitter dopamine (speaking very basically, that's the substance that helps control the reward and pleasure centers of our brains), and they get that by being out and doing things. And dopamine doesn't have far to flow through the brain to reach its target, which allows extroverts to process data quickly, to act and speak under pressure.

Introverts' brains, however, get a little tense when they're flooded with dopamine and are much more happily fueled with a neurotransmitter called acetylcholine. If dopamine is the neurotransmitter of "get up and go," acetylcholine is the neurotransmitter of "settle down and think about it." Acetylcholine also has a long way to go from start to target. Maybe that's why introverts tend to act and react slowly.

But even as we learn more about introversion, we still endure overt and covert pressure to change. In 2010, introverts were riled by a proposal to include introversion in the next edition of the bible of mental health diagnoses, the *Diagnostic and Statistical Manual of Mental Disorders* (DSM-5). Introversion would be one of a number of factors that could contribute to a diagnosis of schizotypal personality disorder. (The proposal describes introversion as "Social Withdrawal: Preference for being alone to being with others; reticence in social situations; avoidance and lack of enjoyment of social contacts/activity; lack of initiation of social contact.")

I understand what they were getting at. Happily, the docs came to their senses and decided to leave introversion out of the discussion. It would have been just one possible component of a multicomponent diagnosis. But they really should have come up with another name for it, or tagged something on top of it: How about Pathological Introversion? Put a little compulsion, desperation into it. 'Cause most of us introverts out here are simply going about normal life with less hubbub than our extroverted friends.

Be assured: You're not mentally ill. You're not dangerous. Or weird. Or lacking in any way. You just like to be alone sometimes. You were born that way.

Quiet Riot

Mild though we may be, it also turns out that introverts are kind of a pissed-off bunch.

I know this because I've seen them online, talking about introversion, relieved to find other people who truly understand, and happy for the opportunity to let their pressure cookers blow. And boy, do they have some steam to let out.

Many introverts have internalized society's message that their way of being is wrong and that extroversion is better. Some have all but given up the fight and let friends and family rearrange them into some semblance of extrovert, however awkward it feels. But when they find other introverts online confirming the validity of their ways, they are first relieved. And then, they get mad.

I've seen introverts accuse extroverts of being shallow and stupid. One reader wrote that she refuses to feel badly "when I'm called 'antisocial' or not 'outgoing' enough or when I refuse to go to a stupid wedding or dull cocktail party . . . My friends and I call this phenomenon the 'tyranny of the extroverts.' "

"I realize that we are a minority in American culture, but why are we the ones who always have to explain ourselves?" wrote another. (Actually, recent research shows that introverts are not a minority—we're about 50 percent of the population.)

And another complained, "Why is it that when an introvert causes a crime he/she is portrayed as a 'loner,' as if that was a terrible thing to be and something to watch out for. If an extrovert commits a crime, they don't say: 'Yes, he/she seemed to be a nice neighbor; but, in hindsight, I thought it was strange that he/she was always talking to someone and always seemed to around other people!' "

Yet another wrote, "I think being called emotionless by my sisters as a child has been one of the most hurtful things that has ever been said to me. Because of my extreme introversion I often appear very calm and disinterested on the outside, even though inside I am often a seething mass of emotion and very interested in what's going on."

With all this frustration and misunderstanding, is it any wonder that we feel like kicking some ass now and then? I've been tempted to pop people in the kisser from time to time when they've gotten all up in my face, trying to drag me out of my shell. They mean well, I'm sure, but I like it in my shell. And if they can't take a pleasant "No, thanks" or "I'm fine" for an answer, then they may not get to enjoy my friendly side.

Of course, extroverts pop up now and then among the online introverts and complain about the hostility they're seeing toward their type. I understand that, too. Who knew that being peppy and friendly and trying to persuade others to get up and boogie in the big party of life could kindle such ire? I try to reassure extroverts that this is something we all just need to get out of our systems. And we do.

And that's fine. A little griping among like souls is cathartic. We're a group that's been kind of beaten down and we need the bravado anger provides before we can settle into quiet confidence. Besides, you can't change what you can't identify, and in venting our spleen we can start pinpointing exactly what makes us feel diminished, bullied, unappreciated, or just plain exhausted. And once we know where and how things feel wrong, we can start righting them in our own minds and in the perceptions of others.

I've been thinking about introversion long enough now that I'm not terribly angry anymore. At the same time, I'm not above correcting people in no uncertain terms when they try to foist their ideas of introversion on me—the shy/anxious or people-hating/misanthropic ideas. No, sirree, that's not me and I'm not taking it anymore.

I don't think anyone has to worry about a bloody uprising of introverts. That's not our style. It's too loud. But there's nothing wrong with letting the world know that we're onto this whole extrovert-bias thing. And we're not staying silent about it anymore. Quiet, maybe. But not silent.

Just Intense Enough

Ever been accused of being "too intense"? Yeah, me, too. I've also been accused of being scary or intimidating. It kinda hurts my feelings.

Part of the reason for this is because introverts are not random smilers. Our default expression tends to be serious and opaque. Of course, smiles are opaque in their own way, but they are the socially preferred mask. Impassive faces are off-putting.

But our real intensity is usually on display in our conversations, and it can knock extroverts on their asses when we unleash it. We're the people who might actually tell the truth when asked, "How are you?" Our questions are not idle, and they require thought and focus. We are inclined toward conversations that require extended eye contact and we like to go deep, sometimes into intense territory.

Some people like that and will plunge into the deep with you right away. Other people back away slowly. Or they flee. You know how that goes—suddenly they see someone across the room and with a wave and a hurried apology, they're gone. That's one way of knowing you were a little too intense.

But what's so bad about intense? So what if we like to express deep thoughts? So what if we think them?

Well, for one thing, rumination has been shown over and over to be a good way to feel lousy, and introverts are nothing if not ruminators. At the very least, we're thinkers, and it's a fine line between thinking and ruminating. Elaine Aron points out that sensitive people's awareness of subtleties and deep processing of information doesn't always work for us. We might go to the doctor with such detailed descriptions of our problems, she wrote, that we sound more like hypochondriacs than people with a legitimate problem. We may take news stories of gloom, doom, and disaster too much to heart. And, she says, because we're so sensitive ourselves to harsh comments, and because criticism can wound us deeply, we couch things in terms so gentle when speaking to others, they might not take us seriously.

Yeah, okay. People do have to say, "I was just kidding," to me a lot. I've been accused my whole life of being "too sensitive." This actually kind of pisses me off, but maybe that's just because I'm too sensitive.

Our intensity is one reason pointless prattle can be intolerable to us. "I absolutely hate listening to superficial small talk and avoid it whenever possible," one introvert seethed. "Yes, I am judgmental about it." That can make social situations stressful, to say the least.

But here's where there's some good news. At least one study finds that substantive conversation does more for our well-being than chatter. In this study, researchers found that the happiest people spent less time alone and more time talking than less-happy people, and they had more than twice as many substantive conversations and one-third as much small talk as the unhappiest people. And that's across the board. Even grumpy, pessimistic people were happier with substantive conversation.

Of course, we don't know if deep conversations cause greater happiness or if happiness causes more deep conversations. It's possible that the cheerier you are the more conversations you attract. Which brings us back around to not smiling and looking intimidating.

But we can live with that. We might not go around with talk-to-me smiles, and we tend to be reserved in large groups, but when we feel comfortable in a small group or one-on-one, we can get plenty of that good-for-you conversation, and we have plenty to say. Sometimes, if truth be told, a little too much. If our intensity tends toward self-disclosure, we can have some pretty awkward getting-to-know-you conversations. Passionate monologues on esoteric subjects also don't work very well, although being intense about ideas is a generally preferable to being intense about what cheese does to your digestion or how your mother almost ruined your life.

Sometimes the best thing to do is try to get other people to be intense about their interests. "Occasionally I might start a small debate on a technicality or a casual opinion on something simple to evoke a deeper connection, to get equal energy out of the other people participating in the conversation," said one introvert—adding that it doesn't always work. "Sometimes I end up frustrated."

Being intense is not a bad thing. It's passion. It's profound. It's philosophical. It can be powerful. And if it scares some people, then too bad for them. On the other hand, we don't have to be intense all the time everywhere with everyone. I say choose your moments, choose your audience, and then take it deep as you please.

The Slow Train of Thought

am terrible at any game requiring speed. My attempts at computer games that involve shooting fast-moving objects turn into frenzied and ineffectual smashing of computer keys. My brain locks, my fine motor skills abandon me. The game lasts seconds. I don't have a chance.

I'm no better at games where you have to come up with a certain number of words in a certain period of time. I come up with words, but other people come up with more. I find this mildly embarrassing, what with my being a writer and all.

Introverts are kinda slowpokey in our thinking. Gears in our heads seem to turn long and ponderously before cranking out an idea. When we're concentrating, we can't easily switch attention from that task to another. An introvert interrupted when deep in work or thought will look up, blinking and groggy, as if being wakened from sleep.

Jung was first to suggest that introverts are deep thinkers.

Eysenck described introverts as phlegmatic. Research has found that introverts have lower thresholds for pain and noise, which gives credibility to Aron's HSP theory as a facet of introversion. Aron looked at brain scans and concluded that some of us take longer to process information because we have particularly sensitive sensory processing systems. Information we take in generates a whole lot of activity in our brains.

Dr. Robert Stelmack, who researches the biological underpinnings of personality, agrees that introverts' sensory processing is more sensitive. That's why we dislike crowds, loud noises, strong smells, he says. But when I told Stelmack my theory—a belief held by many introverts—that introverts are slower thinkers than extroverts, he shot me down. "Speed of cognition is a function of intelligence, not personality," he said. "And the two are not highly correlated."

What he has found, however, is that introverts are slower to act on a thought. Using brain scans, researchers can distinguish between the moment the brain makes a decision, and the moment it tells the body to move in reaction. And while introverts and extroverts were equally quick to make a decision, extroverts were faster at initiating movement. This seems to jibe with Aron's research; when sensitive people looked at a photo to find differences from a previously viewed version, bits and parts all over their brains lit up, indicating deep processing of the information. So while we might not start thinking any slower, we may process more deeply. (Again, this is not necessarily an introvert thing, but is specific to highly sensitive people. There appears to be a lot of overlap between the two, but researchers are still figuring where all the pieces fit together.)

So maybe we're not slow thinkers. Rather, this research suggests, we're slow at translating thought to speech. Also at shooting computerized asteroids. Stelmack says this is also why more extroverts than introverts are athletes, but I think he's talking about a certain kind of athlete. Athletic introverts might be drawn to rock climbing rather than basketball.

No wonder we are so easily steamrolled in conversation. Even if we have something to contribute, between the time we have a thought and the time we start forming words, the conversational moment may have passed. This can be frustrating. Nothing wrong with saying, "Going back to the point you made before . . ." of course, but you don't want to do that all the time, tagging along in the conversation, calling out, "Wait for me!"

Still, our brains are what they are and I wouldn't trade deep thinking for quick thinking. We don't only act slowly, but we are slow to act on the first thought that pops into mind. My brain takes longer to react because it turns things around to examine every angle first. I look at it this way and that way and then the other way before I decide which thought to express.

So we need to allow our brains that room, accept it, and respect it. Let people know when we need to pause for thought. Refuse to let anyone force us into hasty decisions. ("Let me think about that and get back to you.") Choose sports that require careful accuracy rather than quick reactions. And stick to Scrabble for our online gaming.

The Internal Flame

ntroverts might seem dull to some people because we are likely to sit quietly in the corner, speaking little, our faces impassive. But those who slow down, sit down, and look us in the eye might see that our inner flame burns brightly and puts out some heat.

Writing about introverts, Jung said, "From an extraverted and rationalistic standpoint, these types are indeed the most useless of men. But viewed from a higher standpoint, they are living evidence that this rich and varied world with its overflowing and intoxicating life is not purely external, but also exists within. These types are admittedly one-sided specimens of nature, but they are an object lesson for the man who refuses to be blinded by the intellectual fashion of the day. In their own way, they are educators and promoters of culture. Their life teaches more than their words . . . their lives teach the other possibility, the interior life which is so painfully wanting in our civilization."

Oh, Dr. Jung, how you flatter us.

I won't say with certainty that introverts are any wiser or deeper or more spiritual or more creative than extroverts. This is the kind of attitude that causes psychologist Nancy Reeves, author of a book titled *Spirituality for Extroverts,* to call introverts "self-righteous." And I can't argue with her. I'd have to see proof of our superiority in these matters before making a statement so sweeping. But I will say our still waters run deep, and that our external tranquillity is often just a mask for a whole lot of stuff going on under the surface.

Elaine Aron says that sensitive people have active imaginations and vivid dreams. We may have, she suggests, a thin boundary between our conscious and unconscious minds, living with one foot in the real world and one in the world inside our heads. Like so much of our internal busyness, this is both a blessing and a curse.

I love my active imagination; it means I am rarely bored and that given time and psychic space, my creative output can be prolific. A book or movie with compelling emotional content is fuel for my flame long after the experience itself has ended. In fact, I judge a movie's quality by how long it lingers after the lights go up. If it is still feeding my internal flame the next day, it gets my thumbs-up. At museums, I don't try to look at a lot of artwork, but just one or two pieces per gallery—the ones that when my eyes alight on them cause a little flare inside, generate a little heat. These draw me to them and hold me for a long look.

My inner flame is kindled by beauty, natural or man-made. Tree branches against a sky, blackbirds on a winter lawn, a church steeple in the sunset—these are all fuel for the flame. My husband recently pointed out, as we stood on an overlook in Oregon, viewing the Pacific Ocean crashing against the rocks, that places of great natural beauty put a huge, goofy grin on my face. I am alight with pleasure.

But like oxygen can feed a flame, a strong wind may extinguish it. I can't bear a crowded museum. I can only spend a couple of minutes in stores like Abercrombie & Fitch before the loud music and visual stimulation freak me out and drive me away. Movies with lots of explosions and wham-bam action are not only dull to me (Where is the depth? Where are the feeeelings?), but they can be painfully overwhelming. I can't write with music playing. Actually, I can't write with anything going on around me. My husband doesn't understand why I quit working the moment he comes home. But my internal flame flickers with just the slightest breeze from the outside. It burns hot when it is protected, but it is sensitive to outer disturbances.

And so introverts learn to tend our inner flame, closing the door to our office when we need it to burn brightest; fueling it with substantial conversation and meaningful movies, books, and artwork; avoiding as much as possible situations that might overwhelm it.

Given a chance, our inner flame ignites our conversations and kindles our creative output. It is the heat of our passion, which can be hot indeed if given the space and proper fuel. When properly tended, our inner flame lights up not only our lives but the lives of people around us, if they take the time to see it.

What Quiet Says

One of the risks of being quiet is that other people can fill your silence with their own interpretations: You're bored. You're depressed. You're shy. You're stuck-up. You're judgmental. You have nothing to say.

Just as scientists perceive introversion as a void, so does society see our quiet as a hole to be filled by assumptions. Nature abhors a vacuum, and when other people can't read us, they write their own story—not always one we would choose or that's true to who we are.

"[M]y best friend . . . is extremely extroverted and takes my silences and distance as an indication that I am always trying to 'dump' her," one introvert fretted.

Another explained, "I think I'd speak for any introvert when I say if you could hear all the thoughts running through an introvert's mind at any given moment—you'd feel like you'd just had your ear talked off for the last hour."

Seeing what extroverts want is easy: They want contact, they want to be heard, they want as many connections as they can have. That's easy for other people to respond to. Extroverts are rewarded with exactly what they crave. But introverts out in public send ambiguous signals, and this makes some people nervous. They want to give us what we want but don't know what that is. Do we?

Sometimes we want to be at home, but not always. Introverts do have social needs. We don't reject the company of others. (Usually. There are some seriously churlish introverts out there. But I prefer not to equate misanthropy with introversion.) However, we may convince ourselves that we have no need for other people. Perhaps this is self-protection, developed because ever since we were children, extroverts attracted most of the attention. Eventually you stop craving what you can't get.

We may develop prickly defenses to protect ourselves from onslaughts by extroverts determined to break down our boundaries. Or we may use an impenetrable wall of polite smile when we need to check out without being rude. Neither of these makes us appear approachable.

There's a reason the world opens its arms to extroverts but steps cautiously around introverts. Those who do want to connect with us first try to determine, based on our unspoken evidence, what it is we need. Cajoling? Cheering up? To be knocked off our high horse? Then they act accordingly, which, if it isn't what we want, can be annoying or hurtful. And if nothing else, it throws the whole interaction off the track.

That's no good. Surely there is a middle ground where we

may have our quiet space without assumptions made as to our nature. While I don't defend those who make hurtful or negative assumptions about us, we also need to give other people the benefit of the doubt. Like tourists mangling a foreign language, many extroverts are trying to communicate with us but just don't know the language. No need to be Parisian about it and roll your eyes if the effort is well intended. If a question is posed ("Are you angry? Are you bored?"), just answer pleasantly, with a little explanation. ("Don't worry, I'm having a great time in my quiet way.")

If you're misinterpreted more often than not, you might need to give some thought to what your quiet is telling people. When you are sitting quietly, try to parse what kind of quiet you're feeling. "Leave me alone" quiet is different from "thinking hard" quiet, which is different from "enjoying watching the scene" quiet, which is different from "I'm totally overwhelmed, get me out of here" quiet.

Once you have a sense of what you want to project, consider your body language. Maybe that will naturally follow when you identify what you want to say. Or maybe you'll have to practice: This is how I look when I'm enjoying watching the scene; this is how I look when I want to be left alone; this is how I look when I'm open to conversation. If you're sitting with crossed arms and legs, people may see you as closed off, maybe even judgmental. If you lean back, away from the group when everyone else is leaning forward, you might send a rejecting message. And while there's no need to keep a grin on your face, you might do a face check now and then to make sure you're not scowling.

The message, of course, will be subtle. Everything about introversion is. But to live comfortably in the quiet nooks of a noisy world, we have to control our own airspace, and to do that, we have to understand that even quiet says something. We need to make sure it's not sending the wrong messages.

The Fertile Void

Creativity happens when the mind is quiet and receptive. This is the fertile void, where we allow space for invention. And introverts live a life that is halfway there at all times.

Arguments have been made for the superior creativity of introverts. Existential psychologist Rollo May, author of *The Courage to Create*, said that "Genuine creativity is characterized by an intensity of awareness, a heightened consciousness." By that definition, introverts—with our high awareness of the world around us—can perhaps lay claim to higher levels of creativity. And I want to believe that introverts are superior in every way, but I don't know. This is awfully difficult to prove and I'm big on empirical evidence.

Surely extroverts also have access to this higher consciousness. I know at least one extrovert who is wildly creative and applies this creative energy to extrovert endeavors, such as theme parties and Halloween costumes. And where do we place Mozart, who was prolifically creative as well as a flamboyant party boy? Perhaps some of his genius lay in the fact that he had access to both the introvert and extrovert within. One of my personal creative heroes, George Harrison, loved being around other people and was a bit of a hound dog as well. He loved the ladies, who loved him back.

So no, I'm not sure introverts can stake an exclusive claim on creativity. Still, we do seem to have easy access to this place of high awareness, and our aversion to the busy, fizzy world puts us in a position to fall easily into the fertile void.

Psychologist Mihaly Csikszentmihalyi is the father of the influential concept of "flow." This is the state we may reach (on a good day) when we are completely and utterly engaged in a task. Time loses meaning, we forget ourselves, we have great inner clarity, and we do the work for its own sake rather than reward. Csikszentmihalyi studied how creative people work in order to develop his theory. Flow, like introversion, requires an internal focus. In one way, it would seem that introverts live halfway to flow at all times. Maybe it's easier for us to achieve, in our ideal environment. Of course, because we are so sensitive to outer stimulation, we may also be easily jostled out of flow by any outside disturbance. Creative interruptus, as it were.

I asked Dr. Csikszentmihalyi if any research has been done on whether introversion and extroversion have any effect on one's ability to reach and maintain flow. He said there had been no such research, but he continued: "I think that both introverts and extroverts can get into flow, but from doing different things—the first from playing with ideas by themselves, and the second from exchanging ideas or working together with others.

Some people seem to be able to be extroverts at some stage of their work and enjoy interacting, then focus on a problem and enjoy working on it for weeks alone."

Introversion theorist Jennifer Grimes thinks that if it weren't for the ebb and flow of introversion and extroversion within each of us, nothing would ever get done. "If you think about planning and really putting together something in your mind, that could be argued to be introversion," she said "But unless you act and channel the energy outward, then you haven't done anything."

But while talking and doing often are integral to accomplishment, you can't do anything until you have decided what to do, and that's where deep processing comes in. Talking and doing usually occur after some thought has been invested. Talking is, in some regard, the superficial part of communication. Thinking is a quiet and solitary endeavor (even if you are not alone) when a lot of important stuff happens. Watching and thinking and creating and sometimes just letting your mind drift away to daydreams are times when our brains go into relaxed alertness. And in that quiet inner space, brilliant ideas may gestate.

Even if ideas originate in interaction—plenty of people are stimulated by collaboration, and research finds that interaction and serendipity are fuel for innovation—taking a spark of an idea to fruition usually requires that people spend at least a little time inside their own brains, working things out.

I am particularly creative on long road trips, alone or with my husband, once the road has lulled us into silence. A road trip affords hours in the void between places, where I am quiet and removed from familiar surroundings, free to do nothing but watch the road and scenery. In this introspective space, all the ideas that have been tucked in my mind's deepest corners—the little half-formed ones—tiptoe out. They're shy but emboldened by the lack of competition in my brain. In the fertile void, a whisper of an idea can be heard, and the smallest seedling can set roots and grow.

A lot of creativity takes place in solitude as well. Books are written by people locked alone in their offices. (Perhaps nothing has been more detrimental to the production of books than the Internet. You're never completely alone anymore. As if writing didn't take enough discipline, now we have many, many more interesting ways to procrastinate than cleaning out the refrigerator or getting the schmutz out of our keyboard.)

Painting can be more sociable; painting a portrait from a live model is intimate in all sorts of ways, even besides the hanky-panky that has gone on in artists' studios through history. But whatever the relationship between artist and model, when an artist puts brush to canvas, he or she enters the fertile void, where nothing exists but light and color and shape. Painting is a quiet endeavor that requires laser focus. When you see flocks of plein air painters, they might be sitting close together but they are silent, each in communion with an inner muse.

In sleeping, everyone's most introverted state, the brain is left entirely to its own devices. Many notable creative solutions have come to people in dreams: The career-changing American flag painting came to Jasper Johns in a dream. So did the melody of the classic Paul McCartney song "Yesterday," and an experiment that led to the 1936 Nobel Prize in medicine.

The quiet space in which introverts spend much of their time is a natural incubator for art and ideas. But then again, if introverts create great art but never step outside of themselves to share it, does that affect the value of their creativity? Is a spectacular voice heard only in the shower as valuable as a voice heard by thousands? Or hundreds? Or even five?

I don't know the answer, but they're questions worth considering.

That introverts live in the fertile void perhaps supports the notion that we are especially receptive to exploring our creativity. But that same fertile void is accessible to anyone who takes the time to find it. What happens after seeds are planted might be the more important matter.

I Like to Watch

S trictly speaking, the French word "flâneur" is someone who idles or strolls. But the poet Charles Baudelaire put his own shade of meaning on it.

"The crowd is his element," he wrote in 1863, "as the air is that of birds and water of fishes. His passion and his profession are to become one flesh with the crowd. For the perfect flâneur, for the passionate spectator, it is an immense joy to set up house in the heart of the multitude, amid the ebb and flow of movement, in the midst of the fugitive and the infinite. To be away from home and yet to feel oneself everywhere at home; to see the world, to be at the centre of the world, and yet to remain hidden from the world—impartial natures which the tongue can but clumsily define. The spectator is a prince who everywhere rejoices in his incognito."

I was introduced to the word by Dr. Laurie Helgoe, author of

Introvert Power, and I can think of no better description for one of introverts' greatest pleasures: sitting and watching.

I am a flâneur. Many of my best moments of travel have involved sitting and watching. In New York, I spend hours in Central Park, drifting from one bench to another to watch the passing scene. I did the same sitting alone under the long summer sun in the Vigeland sculpture garden in Oslo. In Venice, my husband and I returned several times to a café table under a huge tree, passing hours with snacks and cold drinks, watching Venetians go about their business. In Rome, my niece and I ended every day with gelato at a favorite spot outside the Pantheon. Sitting, eating, watching. Conversation optional.

Sitting and watching is a complete feast for introverts' supersensitive sensory perception. We take it all in . . . the way people walk, how they dress, snippets of conversation. We take the time to notice what a place smells like. I like watching the light change as the afternoon winds down. I try to imagine the homes people are hustling to, heads down, filled with purpose, at the end of the day.

Some extroverted travelers insist that the only way you can know a place is to press flesh and make friends. Introverts disagree. We come to know places in different ways. If you spend two hours visiting with locals at their home, you get an intimate view of a life. If you spend two hours chatting with locals in a pub, you get a peek into another microcosm. But sit in the city or town center for a few hours and you see the ebb and flow of life in a place. You see rich and poor, young and old. You see what people buy and what they eat. You can see how families interact. You see how people dress for work and how they dress for play.

You identify local fads. There is a lot to learn if you sit with your senses wide open.

And introverts are not flâneurs only when we travel. We enjoy being flâneurs at parties, too. If we can't find the kind of conversation we like, or when we are between conversations, we are perfectly content to sit and watch people partying around us. Extroverts often try to pull introverts to the heart of the action, assuming that's where all the fun is. They feel genuinely sorry for us, sitting there on the sidelines and presumably feeling neglected and lonely. Or, they see us and think *dud,* and write us off or tease us. Or they ignore us altogether, which, of the three, is our preferred option.

Because really, we're perfectly happy. We might get a little self-conscious sometimes because of the stigma and assumptions about sitting on the sidelines at a party, but we're not bored or unhappy. We're entertained in our own way. (And when we are no longer entertained, we will either seek out a conversation or go home. We're grown-ups that way.)

Introverts, with pleasure, bear witness to the exploits of extroverts. One introvert said, "I love watching people and extroverts are by far the most fun to watch, so I was always glad to have them around." We don't watch because we long to join the fun. We watch because that *is* the fun.

We are happy to sit alone in restaurants, often carrying a book only as a deterrent against pitying looks and anyone who wants to chat. We are not impatient in airports because these are hives of human activity. Introverts who are not fearful enjoy traveling alone; some would have it no other way. "I am such a travel introvert, I even make my boyfriend and I take separate vacations," one said. "Not all the time, but often, because as an ex-journalist he likes to strike up conversations with people and ask them about themselves and stuff."

Yeah, no need for that.

I suppose you could say that we are merely spectators of life, but that sounds like a put-down. We are not passive, we are engaged, in our own way. This is an art form, a way of life. We are flâneurs, at the center of the world and yet hidden.

Energy In, Energy Out

For the most part, what we "know" about introversion is more theory than fact. Carl Jung talked about energy directed inward versus energy directed outward, and we're on board with that. It feels right. We intuitively know what he's talking about.

But what does it mean, really?

What, exactly, is psychic energy? Can it be scientifically measured in a way that will allow us to ascertain whether introverts and extroverts really do direct it in different directions? And how can we measure the effects of redirecting our psychic energy? What is it that gets tired in introverts when we must behave as extroverts?

We don't know the answers to any of these questions. Not yet. Maybe at some point in the future, brain imaging will find a way to visualize and quantify this. For now, though, it remains in the realm of anecdote.

Nevertheless, it bears thinking about. Four billion introverts (give or take) can't be wrong. We know what it feels like to have our energy drained by too much interaction. It feels like my brain is tired, almost like a muscle would be tired. The more depleted my psychic energy is, the slower my thoughts come, the harder it is to speak full sentences or focus on what's going on around me. My senses become even more sensitive; noise and fuss are more overwhelming. And I become tense, irritated, cranky. That's when I know I need to stop, sit down, let my brain relax and put up its metaphorical feet.

So we know that whatever psychic energy is, we need to manage it. Sometimes that means declining invitations, sometimes it means physically or mentally checking out in situations when we feel ourselves beginning to wilt. Paying attention to the ebb and flow of your energy, and then calibrating it, choosing activities according to whether you have energy in abundance or need a refill, brings equilibrium to life. It also helps you have more fun, since you know when to go and when to stop.

A story: I went to a four-day birding festival. It entailed a lot of interaction and had a busy schedule. As an experiment, I decided not to sign up for any evening events, knowing that by the end of a day of interaction, I'd be wrung out. I was a little conflicted about this—would I miss out? But I gotta be me, so I participated in group events during the day, then retreated to solitude in the evenings.

The experiment was a huge success. I actually made some new, lasting friends that weekend because when I was around people, I was my best self. Escaping into my own head wasn't necessary. I got what I needed by holing up in my hotel room each evening. During daytime activities I had so much fun it didn't even feel like a dog and pony show. It was just fun with no qualifiers.

It was also *my* kind of fun (outdoorsy) with *my* kind of people (birders), which helped. Cognitive scientist Jennifer Grimes theorizes that the real issue is not just how much energy we put out in any situation, but whether we get adequate returns on our energy investment, as I did while birding. (Note: I am not actually a birder. I just like hanging with birders and learning about birds.)

"You'll notice that there is a difference in how exhausted we are in dealing with different kinds of people," Grimes told me. "There are people who like to invest a lot of energy and get a lot back. Some people don't want to invest a lot and don't expect a lot back. The people who are deemed the extroverts in pop literature, the people who are social butterflies, what they get back on an interpersonal level is sufficient for them."

Those of us who are not satisfied by butterfly relationships invest a lot of energy in social situations and require greater returns. For us, interacting in a superficial way is draining and exhausting. It depletes energy but doesn't refill the well with new energy.

Long, thoughtful conversations also require energy, but they replenish it, too. The people I met at that weekend festival were specialists in their field with lots of interesting things to say. A day spent with them left me feeling much more energized than I would have if I'd spent the day on a party boat with a bunch of dudes. That also explains why I can have an hour-long intense conversation at a party and feel pumped up, whereas fifteen minutes of shallow nattering just about sucks the life out of me.

"If what you're putting forth is not commensurate with what you're getting back, there's dissonance," says Grimes. That dissonance is exhausting.

And it would seem to go both ways. As introverts, many of us have at some point been accused of being "too intense." Our intensity can be exhausting to extroverts, who don't put as much into interactions but don't expect as much out of them, either. To extroverts our intensity may feel like pressure to go deeper than they're comfortable with, in a way that depletes their energy.

Some combinations of energy-out/energy-in needs are incompatible. People who don't want to invest a lot but want to get a lot back are draining. They're the emotional vampires. And people who want to invest a lot but take nothing in are the ones who corner you at parties and tell you, in excruciating detail, "The Complete Story of Me."

The energy-in/energy-out equation is imperfect science, if it's science at all. Still, it's a useful construct in deciding where and how to invest your energy. Sometimes you have to consider: What's in it for me?

"We Didn't Know You Were an Introvert, We Thought You Were Just a Bitch."

So said one introvert's brother when she tried to explain introversion to her family over dinner one night.

Not as unkind as it sounds, really. It's based in some truth, though I much prefer the word "bitchy" (behavior) to "bitch" (characterization). But indeed, introverts can come across bitchy or dickish sometimes. We can hardly help ourselves. We're not necessarily naturally like that and we don't get that way for no reason. But admittedly, we can get bitchy when we start running out of energy. And we can get very bitchy if we try to push past our energy lag to keep up with the expectations of extroverts. The bitchy can wash over us suddenly. We're fine, we're fine, we're fine, we're okay, we're kind of okay, we're getting tired, we're getting really tired, *boom*, we're bitchy.

The single most important skill for introverts is managing our energy.

Most of us don't want to hide from life and we like being engaged with the world. But if we can't manage our energy, we are quickly depleted. And when we're depleted, bitchy happens. Managing our energy can help us enjoy social interactions more. If we learn to manage social events so they don't suck the life out of us, we can anticipate them with pleasure rather than dread. When we're comfortable with turning down invitations, we can be more comfortable about accepting them. And when we learn to step away when we feel our energy flagging, we can focus instead on showing our most pleasant selves when we do have the energy.

The first key, of course, is understanding and accepting ourselves as the introverts we are. Like anything else, if you're relaxed and cheerful, you help others feel the same. And all people really want from each other at social events is that everyone smiles and makes nice and likes each other (or at least pretends). So once we understand what we need to function optimally, we then have to learn to defend our boundaries and help others—who might see our withdrawal as rejection—to understand.

Whether or not socializing is your favorite way to spend time is immaterial. To some extent, to be part of society, we all have to go to parties and group outings. We have to spend extended time with family. We have to participate in team efforts. And it's good for us. Being introverted does not mean checking out of the world completely, all the time, forever.

Other people may not understand that when you slip away for a few minutes of quiet time, leave before they want you to, or sit quietly on the sidelines, it's not because you dislike them. It's because you like them and don't want to go all bitchy on them. So it's a matter of first retraining yourself, then others.

You don't even have to tell anyone when you're taking a quiet break. Just disappear for while. People might not even notice. If they do, you can be vague. "Oh, I was around . . ." And now you're ready for whatever is next, and in a far better state of mind than you would have been without a break.

You can, of course, try explaining your introversion and hope others understand. Some will, some won't. If they harangue you, tune 'em out. It doesn't matter what anyone else thinks about whatever you do to manage your energy. We know what we have to do and the more we do it, the more fun everyone has. Eventually people will shrug and accept it as just the way you are. Which is, in fact, true. It is just the way you are, so no need to apologize. Except maybe when bitchy happens.

Magic Words to Plug Energy Drains

ntroverts are capable of many amazing feats, like going to parties, spending holidays with the whole family, attending conferences, and hanging with the gang. But to survive such challenging activities, we have to do whatever it takes to manage our energy and damn the consequences—which are rarely as dire as other people want us to believe.

But with our deep listening habits and our hyperawareness and sensitivity, introverts are particularly susceptible to being sucked into the vortex of other people's demands and expectations, which can cause us to keep going long after we are completely drained of energy. Then we get unhappy, bitchy, and sullen, and the people who talked us into ignoring our own needs wonder what is it with us? Obviously, we hate people.

That's how these ugly stereotypes get started.

So it's up to us to make sure that we don't live down to what other people think they know about us. And in learning to manage my energy better, I have stumbled on some magic words. The words are just as effective for extroverts as introverts, but introverts may need them more. Use these words in your head when you need to resist the pull of other people's expectations. The two versions apply to a variety of situations and nuances.

The magic words are:

Not my responsibility.

Not my problem.

Many introverts are extremely sensitive, even oversensitive, to social messages. Not just from loved ones—from pretty much anyone. Our introvert radars pick up all kinds of messages every which way, and too often, we feel obligated to react to them all. Or at least try. Is it any wonder other people exhaust us? For example: I'm at a dinner party. Things are warming up slowly. Conversation is awkward. An alarm in my head goes off. The party is in trouble! I must come to the rescue! I spring into action, putting on my clown nose and setting plates spinning until everyone is smiling. Then, when everybody else is having fun, I'm exhausted and want to go home.

Was that really my responsibility?

Nope. My only responsibility in any social situation is to be the best me I can, even if it means just being polite, friendly, and pleasant. I don't have to entertain anyone, I don't have to listen deeply to everything everyone says, and I'm not responsible for anyone else's good time. What will be, will be, and everything will be okay.

Oh, and if I don't really want to go a dinner party to begin with, it's not my responsibility to attend. It's my choice. If I choose to decline and somebody's feelings get hurt—well, that's a pity.

But if the only problem I have with not going to the dinner party is that someone else has a problem with it, then that's not my problem. It's that person's problem.

See how that works?

Or consider the chatterbox who corners you with a barrage of words at a party. Even if your introverted deep thoughts see through her chatter to her insecurity and yearning for connection—that's a pity. But it's not your problem. Not unless this is a good friend or beloved family member. Or if you think she's on the ledge *and* you want to fulfill her needs. Otherwise, walk away. Go to the bathroom. She'll live.

These magic words don't work on genuine obligations and legitimate responsibilities toward loved ones (and sometimes even strangers). I don't endorse callous behavior, just boundaries. You have to decide where they are. Sometimes boundaries shift in different situations. That's fine. But when you feel your boundaries being stretched to an uncomfortable degree, do a little reality check. Are you ignoring your own needs to meet someone else's? Do you want to?

If not, whisper to yourself the magic words.

Not my responsibility.

Not my problem.

And you know their real magic? Used properly, these words can help us enjoy social occasions more than we ever thought possible by plugging unnecessary energy drains: the stuff that is not our responsibility and not our problem.

Introverts Are Not Failed Extroverts

ntroversion is often treated as the space where extroversion is
not. It's treated as a vacuum. An absence rather than a presence.

This has particularly been true in the study of personality
psychology. In that field, the five stable traits, called the Big Five,
are Openness, Conscientiousness, Extroversion, Agreeableness,
and Neuroticism. Researchers measure these traits with question-
naires of positively and negatively weighted items. If you answer
yes to a positively weighted item, it indicates extroversion. If you
answer no, it indicates lack of extroversion—or, scientists assume,
introversion.

Such a very inexact science. Sloppy, even.

I looked at the IPIP-HEXACO extraversion measuring tool,
which measures four facets of extroversion: Expressiveness, Liveliness, Sociability, and Social Boldness. Each of the facets in this

questionnaire is measured by brief descriptions of feelings or behaviors, weighted positively or negatively.

Let's look at some of the items in the questionnaire. Under the topic of Expressiveness, "Bottle up my feelings" is weighted negatively, so if you answer yes, it means you're less extroverted and therefore more introverted. But is that right? Seems to me that introverts in their element—a quiet place with trusted people— are less likely to mask our feelings than extroverts in their element, surrounded by hubbub. Introverts are no more or less open with our feelings than extroverts, as long as we're with people who take the time to listen. So in this case, the absence of this behavior doesn't really say anything about extroversion versus introversion.

Under Social Boldness in the questionnaire, "Would be afraid to give a speech in public" is also negatively weighted.

Nope, that's not right, either. I'm comfortable speaking in public, as are lots of introverts. The sense of being in control can make public speaking pretty easy for us. We know what we're there for and what we want to say. So that doesn't tell us anything about introversion, either.

The Social Boldness section of the questionnaire also suggests that non-extroverts "Have little to say." Well now, that's just rude. Sez who? We have plenty to say under the right circumstances. Yes, extroverts talk more, but "have little to say" sounds a little value-judgment-y to me and I flat-out reject it as a description of introversion.

The questionnaire then turns to Sociability. "Rarely enjoy being with people" is, of course, negatively weighted. Say yes and you're less extroverted and therefore more introverted. But that's wrong, too. It depends entirely on what people, how many, and how long, doesn't it? If the item read, "Rarely enjoys being with large groups of people having a loud, rollicking good time," then maybe I'd allow it. Although sometimes I even enjoy that, especially if I am free to sit quietly and watch the hubbub.

Among the items related to Liveliness, "Feel that I have a lot of inner strength" is positively keyed, making it an extroverted quality. Really? That's just cockamamie. What does inner strength have to do with introversion or extroversion? This one is hard to even argue. Best just to ignore it.

Introversion is so much more than what extroversion isn't. But in this measure all the qualities that imply introversion have a sad-sack tone: *Seem to derive less enjoyment from interacting with people than others do. Keep in the background. Speak softly. Find it difficult to approach others.*

The positively weighted—or extroverted—qualities, however, are full of vigor: *Have leadership abilities. Love to chat. Am the life of the party.* And let us note, by the way, the subtle implication of introvert traits being *negatively* weighted. Sure, it's just the language of statistics, but somehow it all seems to add up to a big raspberry. Measuring introversion as the lack of extroversion suggests that extroversion is something and introversion is a sort of nothingness. It is a lack. A hole. A place where something isn't.

I reject that. I believe introversion does have its own energy, its own being.

Consider this: In the course of doing his research on happiness and extroversion, psychologist Will Fleeson, PhD, had a bunch of college students sit at a table and assigned them to act either introverted or extroverted for ten minutes at a time.

Surprisingly, the introverts behaving extroverted weren't the most pooped after ten minutes. No, it was the extroverts who were most exhausted, by the effort of behaving introverted.

Maybe extroversion is a force so strong that suppressing it is exhausting. Maybe introverts just have a lot of experience in acting extroverted, so the exercise required less effort for them. Or maybe introversion generates energy of its own that is more than extroverts can handle. Our secret superpower. One thing is for sure, though—if introversion is that exhausting, it sure as hell isn't nothing.

I Like People, Just Not All People All the Time

Except for the misanthropes among us (and there are probably misanthropic extroverts, too), introverts are not anti-people, as some people infer. That's quite a leap to make, isn't it? I don't eat tuna salad every day, that doesn't mean I'm anti–tuna salad. If I wanted to get persnickety about it, I could make a case that introverts are more genuinely people-oriented than extroverts because we're always on the lookout for connections and conversations, whereas extroverts are content with noise and chatter.

"The problem with groups is I find the number of people you talk to is inversely proportional to the level of intimacy you're able to achieve with each member," one introvert said. "More than two or three people and everyone just seems to be talking over themselves to get themselves heard."

Either way, introverts do like people but in controlled doses and small numbers. We like spending one-on-one time with good friends. I need that as much as I do solitude. Introverts don't get lonely if they don't socialize with a lot of people, but we do get lonely if we don't have intimate interactions on a regular basis. (And I don't mean sex, though that's good, too.) Sometimes we like being around people without actually interacting with them. Humanity is endlessly fascinating, even if people are often boring.

Some people enjoy talking to anyone, anytime. I have a friend who strikes up conversations with strangers everywhere we go. This is actually kind of irritating, but it's none of my business. I respect her right to be an extrovert. But I suppose you could accuse me of being a snob in this regard: Shared membership in the human race is not enough commonality to make anyone and everyone interesting to me. While, of course, you never know until you start a conversation who is interesting and who isn't, I see no compelling reason to try to locate every interesting person in the world through random conversation. Chances are pretty good you'd have a thousand pointless conversations for every excellent one.

Nonetheless, finding some individuals dull or even just unnecessary to my life is not the same thing as disliking all people. There's absolutely nothing wrong with finding our own thoughts more interesting than a long story about someone's husband's niece's gum surgery.

Introverts also don't want to socialize every day. Every social interaction drains a little bit of energy, and after a few consecutive days of socializing, we need to shut down. After days of interacting, my brain feels stuffed with other people's words. They rattle and chatter and knock around and I want to shake them out my ears. That's when I turn down even invitations I might otherwise accept. When I've hit the wall of socializing, no invitation sounds like as much fun as being alone.

Our limited ability to socialize causes us to be selective about whom we see when, and how. We are reluctant to squander precious social energy on empty-calorie encounters. Admittedly, we can be unfriendly—if you consider declining to engage with people unfriendly. But this is not from hostility toward others as much as it is a form of self-protection and self-regulation.

There's nothing wrong with declining to join every party, deciding not to talk to everyone who crosses your path, choosing quality over quantity in your relationships. It just means that you know your limits and choose to save yourself for people and activities that matter. Other people might think that means you don't like people, but what it really means is that you only make time for people you like.

Don't Call Us, We'll Call . . . Well, No, Maybe We Won't

The telephone.

Ah, the telephone.

Nine out of ten introverts agree: The telephone is the tool of the devil.

Why do we hate the phone? Oh, so many reasons.

"Phones are like spoiled brats . . . *Stop what you're doing and pay attention to me right now!*" one introvert griped. "I hate being bossed around by a gadget."

Because we think deeply and act slowly, you can practically hear the tearing of neurons when the phone rings and we try to pull our minds away from the task at hand to focus on whoever is insisting we jump to it *right now*! It's like being wakened from a dream by a shrieking alarm, and we struggle to focus on a disembodied voice and whatever he or she has to say, which is, let's face it, not always particularly interesting.

And the jangle of a phone causes a flood of dopamine, the

get-up-and-go neurotransmitter that extroverts crave but that can make introverts feel overwhelmed and anxious.

Like a lot of introverts, I also don't have a chance on the phone with a chatterbox and end up doing a lot of listening and uh-huhing. Is it any wonder we get bored and restless? "I have an outgoing friend who, when she calls, tells me all about everything going on in her life, while I can barely get a word in edgewise," one introvert complained. "And since she is far away, and doesn't 'do' email, it's about the only way we can catch up."

Introverts' tendency to think and respond slowly leads to long pauses, which are awkward on the telephone. Or they sound like invitations for the other person to keep talking. And when I try to just plunge in and chatter, I often careen out of control with stream-of-consciousness riffs that eventually confuse even me, until I sputter to a stop, disconnected thoughts and anecdotes and explanations drifting to the ground around me. Have I confused the other person as much as I confused myself? No telling because we have so little to go on. There's no "text and subtext, body language" as one introvert put it. "I can't 'place myself' properly (if that makes sense), when it's not face-to-face."

A boring or too-long phone call makes me feel trapped and desperate. Worse, callers often pick up on my impatience and unhappiness. No offense is intended. I might be perfectly happy to spend hours talking to this person face-to-face. My impatience is with the medium, not the message. I just give bad phone. Even my husband hates talking to me on the telephone. He's never pleased to hear the telltale clickety-click of computer keys when the conversation is over for me, whether it is or not for him. Even when I refrain from typing, he can tell when I've checked out by the sound of my voice.

Hurting other people's feelings is a risk we take when we let the phone bully us into answering. One introvert said she ignores the phone unless it's someone she absolutely needs to talk to at that moment. Otherwise, she returns the call later, "when I safely can, without the caller knowing I am cranky just because I have to talk/listen."

To make it worse, phone aversion is often treated as a moral failing. People seem to believe that if we were good people who love our friends and family, we would enjoy talking on the phone with them.

But love has nothing to do with it. Phone calls are not the best way for many of us to feel connected with people. The trouble is, one introvert said, "we can sit in complete silence with another human being and still feel connected to them. On the phone, there's pressure to fill the silence whether or not you have anything to say."

"It's a huge chasm, leaping to meet the person on the other end of the line emotionally/communicatively" is how another described it.

Lots of us are fine with email and texting, which we find efficient and which allow us to think at our own pace. "Most of my friends lovingly tease me about hating the phone so much and texting has become our primary tool for communication," one introvert wrote. "Because of this I know that if one of my close friends is calling, it's because it's actually important and/or time-sensitive and I find it easier to respond appropriately."

Giving up the phone altogether is not feasible. I have far-flung friends with whom my phone conversations get deep and philosophical. These calls keep the friendship vibrant. But a call like that can derail my whole day. So I try to schedule those calls. Friends resisted at first, but they got used to it.

Phone calls are much easier if I wear a headset and keep my hands free. Holding a phone in my hand for a long conversation makes me feel as shackled physically as I am mentally. With a headset, I can do simple chores, such as sweeping or washing dishes, while I talk. Even simple computer games such as Tetris and FreeCell can help me focus by keeping the restless part of my mind busy.

Technology has provided lots of tools to make the phone tolerable. Or at least less intolerable. We have caller ID, we can assign different ringtones for different people so we feel less ambushed, and we can decide whether or not we want to answer at that moment. "And best of all it has an Off switch!" one introvert said.

Video calls can be more fun than torture, although I definitely prefer to schedule those, so I can be properly dressed, put on a little makeup, look nice. It is, in a way, a face-to-face visit.

The texting introvert above also wrote that she and her equally phone-averse mother have agreed to talk on the phone weekly. After all the catching up is done and they start just getting silly, one or the other will say, "I'm done being on the phone now so I'm going to go, but we'll check in again next week?"

"It is such a relief to be able to be this honest and not have to worry about hurt feelings or misunderstandings!" the introvert said. "I've begun to try this line with other people in my life and surprisingly, it's going over well."

There is a special place in heaven for the people in our lives who accept, even if they don't share, our aversion for the telephone. I appreciate faraway friends who are fine with scheduling calls. I am grateful to people who know when to end a call. I even appreciate people who generally respect my phone aversion but also know when to tell me that it's time to take a conversation from email to the telephone. Sometimes I need a nudge, and that's okay, too. We're all in this together and we don't need things our way all the time.

Interestingly, society may actually be taking a turn toward our way of thinking. According to Nielsen, we're making fewer phone calls than we used to (we peaked in 2007), and in 2008 it reported that people were sending and receiving more texts with their mobile phones than they were making or receiving phone calls.

Either the entire world is having a moral crisis or lots of people feel about the phone the way we do. They just didn't admit it because they didn't want to be accused of not loving enough.

We Gotta Fight for Our Right Not to Party

For all introverts have in common, we also are each a unique stew of personality and experiences, nature and nurture. No two of us are alike. (Some like karaoke. I rest my case.) And so to live life the introvert's way, we need to figure out the basics of our own nature and how to calibrate our need for solitude with our need for human interaction.

Do you recognize the nuances of your own burnout? When you're starting to hit the wall in social interaction, would just an evening alone do the trick, or do you need a weekend? Would ducking into the bathroom help, or is it time to go home? Are you tired of the party or just tired of the chatterbox who shows no sign of winding down? Do you want to stay home tonight because you want to stay home or because you have succumbed to inertia?

Energy management is key to an introvert's life outside the house, because by respecting our own limits and managing our energy, we can enjoy socializing more and minimize the risk that we'll sulk or snap. Sometimes getting people to understand that can be difficult. They love a party and they can't understand why everybody doesn't.

Don't you want to be with me?

You can't go home now!

But it won't be the same without you!

You're such a party pooper!

People who don't dance are bad in bed!

(That last is a true story, reported by an introvert who was mortified by this accusation made by a near stranger at a party.)

Extroverts are as indoctrinated as introverts to believe that extroversion is healthy and introversion is shameful. So you can't really blame them for wanting to save us from ourselves. Their intentions are often good. But we don't need saving, and it's up to us to somehow get that across in a loving but firm manner. Retraining others to accept our need for space can be difficult.

But the bottom line is this: Parties are supposed to be fun, and if you don't have fun and have no other compelling reason to make an appearance ("because others say I should" is not a reason), then there is no logical reason to go. And that goes for a lot of things. Yes, there are certain horrendous activities that we have no choice but to suffer through (such as team-building exercises at work), but if something that is supposed to be fun doesn't sound like fun to you, then declining the invitation is A-OK.

Now, some extroverts who plead for our participation genuinely want our company. Others just want us to join the more in their merriment. And still others, I suspect, see implied judgment in our position and think that merely by declining to participate in something, we are condemning it.

In some cases, no explanation is necessary. Not everybody needs to understand and appreciate the nuances of your personality. When we're talking about acquaintances or casual friends, you owe them only good manners. If you don't want to join the fun, you say thanks but no thanks. When it's time to go home, you say good-bye. No apologies, no overexplaining. If they huff and puff, or wail in despair, take a step back. Not your problem. As long as you're not throwing a monkey wrench into any plans, you are entitled to control your own time. And no, *"It won't be the same without you!"* is not the same thing as throwing a monkey wrench in their plans. Just assure them that it will be close enough.

But because we care, we do factor in the needs of friends and loved ones as we start staking out our quiet turf. We're not trying to hurt anyone's feelings. Close friends and family might require, and deserve, more. You can explain to them about managing your energy, assure them that by doing this you'll be more fun to be around, tell them it has nothing do with how much you love them. Tell them that last bit over and over if you have to, until it sinks in.

And then, do what you gotta do. Retraining is an incremental process, but every time you excuse yourself from the house to take a walk, or leave when the party is just getting heated up, or drink that first cup of morning coffee in your bedroom instead of with the family, you retrain people to expect that of you.

Not only that, but every time you join the crowd again, with a smile and a new attitude, they start making the connection between you going away and you coming back better. Eventually, they might start recognizing the signs that you're reaching your limit and voluntarily clear you a little space, like parents might suggest nap time to a cranky toddler. Don't take this personally. Accept it gratefully because at this point, your quiet fight is over. You have staked out your right to be an introvert.

Loneliness Is a State of Mind

A lot of people confuse being alone with being lonely.

Even Merriam-Webster gets it wrong. Look up "lonely" and the first definition is "being without company." But really, who uses it that way? If someone called and asked if you were with anyone, would you say, "No, I'm lonely"? That would send the entirely wrong message and the person calling would feel sorry for you. Worse, that person might come running to be with you, which is a lovely gesture but, let's face it, could spoil perfectly good alone time. (Actually, an introvert enjoying alone time probably wouldn't even have picked up the phone. But that's another chapter.)

Look up "alone" in the dictionary and the first definition is "separated from others," which sounds a lot lonelier than the definition of lonely. "Separated from others" implies that you were with others, but now you are not. There's an air of loss about it.

Aloneness is an external condition: a person without other

people. Loneliness is an internal state. It is a longing to be with other people. Loneliness is about how you feel about being alone.

Much of the time, introverts feel pretty good about being alone. We can drive for hours with no more company than the radio. "I'd spend a fortune and hours of my time to avoid carpooling," one introvert wrote. We can spend a weekend at home alone and not get bored. We love evenings alone. Also mornings. We consider nothing to do something to do. "I love waking up in the morning to an empty room after my roommate has gone to class," wrote another introvert. "I get to lie in bed, drink coffee, and watch an episode of *House*."

Sartre did not say, "Hell is other people at breakfast," no matter how many people on the Internet attribute it to him. However, introverts say it all the time. Morning chatter is exceedingly difficult for us.

Introverts' need for copious amounts of time alone is one reason we don't have a million friends. Friendships require time to maintain, and too many friendships take too much time. But numbers of friends are irrelevant to loneliness.

The UCLA Loneliness Scale, which researchers use to detect loneliness, doesn't ask anything about numbers of friends or the amount of time you spend with people. It doesn't ask people to rate themselves according to whether they live by the credos "the more the merrier" or "I never met a stranger." Ratings are more along the lines of "How often do you find yourself waiting for people to call or write?" and "How often do you feel shut out and excluded by others?"

Being lonely is never good. Being alone is not always bad.

I like the word "solitude." Solitude implies tranquillity. It sounds restful and inviting. I picture a lone tree on a hill, or a cozy armchair on a snowy day, or a little cabin under a big Montana sky. Solitude sounds good and healthy and not the least bit pathetic.

Or, to put a jauntier spin on it, I like "going solo." I like going to movies solo and just ignore pitying looks directed my way. Those people might as well feel sorry for someone else. Maybe that woman on the horrible first date. Or the guy who was dragged to a chick flick by his wife. Or the woman whose chatty friend insists on providing running commentary. I've got Milk Duds and a comfy seat and nobody pestering me. I couldn't be happier. I'm not lonely. I'm just going solo.

Introverts are not immune to loneliness. We can be lonely surrounded by people if we haven't found anyone to connect with. We also can get lonely if we allow the momentum of solitude to override our natural need for companionship. Being alone is always easiest for introverts; it is the path of least resistance. It's up to us to recognize the signs within ourselves that we have been too isolated for too long. When we start feeling blue. When we start feeling lonely.

Introverts are actually kind of vain about our appreciation for solitude. We don't make a big deal about it, but we consider the ability to spend time alone as a marker of an interesting person, an individual of substance. Of course, we would sound a little bit cracked if we urged people to spend more time alone, unlike people who tell us we should get out more. But just smile when they say that. Their hearts are in the right place. People might worry that you're lonely, and it's kind of them to care. But you can be confident that if you don't feel lonely, being alone is just fine.

The Happiness Bias

R esearchers insist on insisting introverts are unhappy. I don't think we are but even if we aren't, a body of research correlating extroversion and happiness seems designed to make us so.

For example, one 2010 study tells us that everyone is happier when they act like extroverts. This doesn't explicitly exclude introverts because we can, after all, behave like extroverts when we choose. And certainly that can make life easier for us in certain circumstances. And to some people we might look a lot happier when we behave like extroverts than we do when we're sitting quietly behaving like introverts. Nevertheless, is it really correct to say that we *are* happier when we're acting like an extrovert?

I called the lead researcher on this particular study, psychologist Will Fleeson, PhD, of Wake Forest University, to talk about this.

"One of the things my research has shown is that people are

far more flexible than they realize, and almost all people actually exhibit levels of most traits in their everyday behavior," Fleeson explained. "The difference between introverts and extroverts turns out to be in moderately extroverted and introverted behaviors. Extroverts do moderately more extroverted behavior slightly more often, and introverts do moderately more introverted behavior slightly more often."

Okay. First: Note that he is talking about behavior—or the *state* of extroversion, from which he differentiates the *trait* of extroversion, which is the inborn inclination. And this particular finding only confirms that introverts who are not shy are perfectly capable of behaving extroverted when they choose. We knew that. But Fleeson's research also suggests that even those of us with trait introversion are happier when we are behaving like extroverts.

Fleeson conducted several studies where he had students, at various intervals, record how extroverted they were behaving and how happy they felt. And he found a strong correlation between acting extroverted and feeling happy—in both people who measured high and those who measured low in trait extroversion. (As usual, introversion was only measured in relationship to extroversion—people who measured high in extroversion were assumed to measure low in introversion, and vice versa.)

But Fleeson's research, when I started delving into it, ended up suggesting different questions than the ones initially asked.

The first thing Fleeson explained to me is that he used a very specific scientific definition of extroversion. None of Jung's energy-in/energy-out stuff. Instead, he had people describe how they were feeling in words he says are most consistently used to

describe extroversion: talkative, enthusiastic, assertive, bold, energetic. He also used a specific set of words to describe positive
affect (science-speak for looking happy): excited, enthusiastic,
proud, alert, interested, strong, inspired, determined, attentive,
active.

But wait a minute! Aren't those kind of extrovert-centric descriptions of both feelings and happy behavior? What about the
introvert version of the same things?

Where is it written that being assertive, for example, means
you're behaving like an extrovert? Introverts can be assertive.
Speaking quietly can be quite effective. We can be energetic and
talkative in conversations that engage us, although most of us
agree that there's a good deal too much empty chatter going
on in the world. Is that acting extroverted? Maybe. Or maybe
only small-talk talkative is behaving like an extrovert, whereas
intense-talk talkative is behaving like an introvert. Both talkative, just different.

And don't *even* suggest that introverts aren't passionate. The
greatest paintings, literature, and scientific revelations were
likely born in a quiet room. Introverts are all full of passion; it
just tends to seethe within.

Even more annoying are the words he had his research subjects
use to describe positive affect: excited, enthusiastic, proud, alert,
interested, strong, inspired, determined, attentive, active. Where
are introvert-centric terms such as peaceful, content, engaged, en-
grossed, focused, amused, composed, and calm?

And what is enthusiasm? Does it have to be bubbly and force-
ful? Introverts can be enthusiastic, too, even if we don't display it
by dancing into rooms. If you take the time to look, the introvert

version of enthusiastic might be the way our eyes light up when something excites us, like the aforementioned goofy grin I get when viewing a place of great natural beauty.

In fact, in designing his study, Fleeson used a common three-legged stool description of happiness used by researchers: But he used only one leg of that stool—positive affect, which is all those energetic, excited, enthusiastic words. It's the kind of "happy" other people can see: visible, external, noisy happy.

Fleeson didn't include in his research the second leg of the stool, which is life satisfaction. This one is more cognitive than emotional. It's knowing that even if you're not feeling great at the moment, your life is pretty good all around. And the third leg of the stool is absence of negative affect—*not* having anxiety, fear, anger, or frustration, which would mean you felt calm and at peace with the world. And that kind of affect says "introverted" to me.

But Fleeson didn't use that leg in his research, and so one could argue that words describing introvert happiness are not even included in the way Fleeson measured happiness.

So Fleeson's happiness stool is all caddywumpus. It's tilted toward extrovert-style happiness.

And here's another take on the extroversion-happiness equation: Maybe extroverts seem happier because they do everything bigger.

Psychologist Donna McMillan, PhD, found that when completing various measures frequently used in psychological research, such as the Likert-type scale (that's the "on a scale of one to ten" kind of measurement), extroverts were more likely to choose extreme answers than introverts. So, for example, if asked to rate on a scale of one to five how happy they are, extroverts are more likely to choose *five! wheeee!* than introverts.

Maybe this is because extroverts are genuinely happier than introverts. Or maybe, McMillan suggested, it's because extroverts seem to require more cortical stimulation than introverts, and circling a whoop-de-doo five is more stimulating than choosing a ho-hum four. So we don't know whether extroverts' happiness actually is cranked up to five, or if just their way of communicating it is.

I have no argument with the research in this regard: If you want to feel that happy-doodle kind of energetic happiness, you can get there by being outgoing, enthusiastic, and talkative. I'll buy that. If we act externally energetic and outgoing, we'll feel energetic and outgoing. William James proposed essentially the same thing in the 1880s, theorizing that emotion follows behavior. But is that the kind of happy we want all the time? That kind of happiness is fleeting, and happiness that requires the participation of other people is doubly so.

What would happen if introvert-style happy words were added to the research? That would change a lot. Quite possibly, science would show that introverts are just as happy as extroverts, in our own soft-spoken way.

Who's a Narcissist?

Even introverts worry sometimes that their inner focus makes them narcissists. Sigmund Freud said we are. So do other people. "My mother just keeps saying it's just a form of selfishness, get over it," one introvert complained.

This accusation is tangled up in the misperception that shyness and introversion are the same. Shy people are accused of narcissism because of their fear that everyone watches their every move. But is this accurate? Is introversion narcissistic? Is shyness?

First of all, we have to differentiate between "overt narcissism"—which is the grandiose, self-absorbed narcissism that leaves lives in shambles—and "covert narcissism," which is vulnerable and anxious.

Covert narcissism is "anxious self-preoccupation," says psychologist Jonathan Cheek, who cocreated a widely used scale—

the Cheek and Buss scale—to measure shyness. "It's not like the person is impulsively or aggressively indulging a preference for oneself. Both kinds of narcissism are excessive self-focus, but I think the distinction is very important."

Though Cheek researches shyness, which, as we have already established, is not the same as introversion, his research is worth taking a look at, to try to fit it into our understanding of introversion.

The Cheek and Buss scale finds that shy people are highly unlikely to be overt narcissists. They might wrestle with covert narcissism, but that's harder on them than on anyone around them. So it's not entirely wrong to accuse shy introverts of narcissism, of a kind. Just not a kind that should trouble anyone else.

Whereas overt narcissism—a destructive combination of charm, entitlement, and lack of empathy—leaves a trail of tears, covert narcissists are just timid. Scolding them doesn't accomplish anything useful. (Scolding overt narcissists doesn't accomplish anything, either, but for other reasons.) And they don't deserve it. They know they're self-conscious and they're not having any fun.

And not-shy introverts? The narcissist label doesn't stick on us at all. We don't feel like everyone is watching us, nor do we demand that they do.

I suppose people associate introversion with narcissism because we spend so much time in our own heads, as if we can't get enough of ourselves. In a way, yeah, that makes sense. But even in our own heads, we're not necessarily ruminating on ourselves. We're thinking about all sorts of stuff. We might even be paying attention to everything going on around us even though we're not interacting with any of it. Maybe our quietness allows us to actually pay more attention to what's going on around us.

And, least narcissistic of all, we don't necessarily want attention. We don't sit silently in order to bait people into drawing us out. We're not fishing. We're sitting quietly because that's what we do. Some people misinterpret this as sitting in silent judgment of everyone on the (literal and metaphoric) dance floor. It makes them nervous, or even angry or hostile. That's when they start flinging accusations, like calling us narcissists.

We're not.

If you don't feel like all eyes are on you all the time, you aren't suffering covert narcissism. If you don't want all eyes on you all the time, you aren't an overt narcissist. If anyone tries to slap that label on you, just put up your self-confident force field and let the accusation bounce right off.

Actually, there can be made an argument for extroverts as the narcissists. After all, they're the ones who need to charm everyone around, who think their slightest utterances are worth uttering, who thrive on attention. That seems at least as narcissistic as sitting quietly and liking your own company.

All narcissism isn't bad. Narcissism can be adaptive—that is, healthy. Adaptive narcissism contributes to extroverts' confidence and charisma. Introverts also make good use of that kind of narcissism when we put on our extrovert faces. And it's the kind of narcissism we indulge every time we decide our own company is more interesting than any other options before us at the moment.

Maybe we've all got a little narcissist in us; it helps us get up every day and do what we must in this world. Sure, narcissism can go bad, creating con men on the extroversion side, and misanthropes among the introverts. Nevertheless, introverts are no more or less likely than extroverts to be narcissists. Equating narcissism and introversion is flawed logic. You might be a narcissist. But if you are, it's as well as, not because of, your introversion.

Turning the Extrovert Advantage Upside Down

You've probably heard that extroverts have the advantage in all kinds of venues. They do better socially. They find mates more easily. They succeed professionally. They make better leaders. They suffer less stress. Less depression. They're more optimistic. They have better memories. One study even suggests they're stronger and better-looking, since good-looking babies are rewarded with more attention, which causes them to respond by being more outgoing.

It's enough to discourage even the proudest introvert. What can we do in the face of scientific evidence of our disadvantages?

Blow it off.

First of all, the advantages are entirely a cultural construct. Maybe extroverts have it all going on in North America, but that's just one slice of the world. One study found that in China, children considered sensitive and quiet are popular among peers, but in Canada, that type of child is less likely to be popular. So clearly, extroversion is only an advantage in some cultures.

But even in our more extrovert-friendly society, you can turn every extrovert advantage into a disadvantage. And vice versa.

I don't suggest introversion is better than extroversion. But I bristle at the suggestion that extroversion is better than introversion.

For example, that memory thing? One study I read suggests that introverts are more susceptible to false memories than extroverts. When given a list of related words (table, sit, legs, seat, couch) and then asked to recall them, introverts were most likely to add, for example, "chair" to the list, since it relates to the other words although it was not included on the list.

Sounds pretty thoughtful to me. Creative, even. Maybe extroverts are more literal and don't see beyond what's right in front of their faces. Maybe they're less intuitive.

Perhaps extroverts do suffer less stress. Maybe it's because they don't think about stuff as hard as introverts do. Or maybe it's because they are rewarded for being their natural selves, while introverts are urged to be someone different (namely, extroverts).

Are extroverts less depressed? Okay, it's hard to find much positive to say about depression, but if it's a price some of us have to pay for thinking and feeling deeply, then we just have to learn to manage it. I'm a big believer in the yin and yang of life. Happiness is all the sweeter if you've been sad. And sadness is often a first step toward enlightenment. (Deep, right?)

Perhaps extroverts have more friends. No surprise there,

since introverts don't desire as many friends. But if an extrovert claims, "No such thing as too many friends!" does that also imply that there are never enough? Are they perpetually falling short of having enough? Introverts might have four friends and feel like that is more than enough. Could that mean that the introvert is actually more successful at friendship? Just something to think about.

Professional success? That extroverts are more professionally successful is one of those pieces of common wisdom that's not so wise. Do they earn more money? Ask introvert Warren Buffett. Are they more famous? Ask introvert Steve Martin. Perhaps they are more likely to crow about their success or to put themselves in the public eye so that people can see their success. But then we're talking about visibility, not measurable success.

And if you consider that sort of visibility a measure of success, does it then follow that it also is a measure of failure? If someone high profile crashes and burns, is that a bigger failure than someone who crashes and burns quietly?

A 2006 article in *USA Today* pointed out that four in ten top executives are introverts. A more recent study out of Harvard found that while extroverted leaders are effective leading teams of passive (also defined as less extroverted in this study) employees, proactive employees need a different kind of leader—an introverted one. Extroverted leaders might feel a little threatened by a team that has its own ideas. Employees in this study felt that the extroverted leaders were not particularly receptive to their ideas. An extroverted leader and a team of extroverts might do a lot of jockeying for position, for center stage, as it were. But, to extrapolate from this research, it seems an introverted leader would not only be open to ideas from an extroverted team but would then be better at taking all those ideas off into a quiet cave to sort through and assess them.

Here is that yin and yang again. Steve Jobs was an extrovert, his partner Steve Wozniak an introvert. Together, without exaggeration, they changed the world.

The extrovert advantage is a false construct, a measurement taken with an extrovert ruler. If we start measuring by an introvert ruler, we would find extroverts falling short. What if you started counting substantial thoughts versus bland niceties expressed each day? Introvert advantage. What if you measured time spent productively alone versus time spent in frivolous pastimes with others? Introvert advantage. What if well-written emails were considered more valuable than meandering phone calls? Introvert advantage.

Extroverts don't have the advantage in everything. Introverts have got it going on, too. We just don't like to boast.

The Party Predicament

f parties were roller coasters, extroverts would be the riders with their arms in the air squealing *wheeee!*, and introverts would be the ones hanging on with a white-knuckled grip.

Some introverts loathe parties without apology and simply refuse invitations. That's okay. I get it. They have no predicament. No parties, no problem.

But I don't completely hate parties and I consider them a social contract we make with friends. Attending friends' parties is among the kindnesses we extend to those who are kind enough to throw them. Having given parties myself, I am fully familiar with the "what if no one comes?" terror, and the letdown when friends don't show. So when friends throw parties, I usually attend and make every effort to fulfill my duties as a guest. I might not stay long, and sometimes I fall down on the job, but I try.

Big parties can be tough, but sometimes you have to man up. Weddings and other milestone events come to mind. Fortunately, if a party is really big, you can stay only as long as it takes for the host to notice you're there. I've gone to parties where I didn't stay as long as it had taken me to put on my party frock and makeup. Other times I've found a small party within the big party and stuck with that. As far as I'm concerned, mingling is not mandatory at parties.

But I once attended a big, festive wedding party for a friend's daughter, and shut down. I walked into the cacophonous room full of happy strangers and went catatonic. It was a terrible experience for me. I was awkward, my small talk was stilted, I was unintentionally rude. I forgot people's names, clung to the couple I'd come with, and fled as soon as I could.

I'm not always that bad at parties, but you never know when it's going to happen. Consequently, I approach parties with trepidation.

I don't go to parties to meet new people but to enjoy festivities with people I know. That's why throwing parties is fun. I know almost everyone there and have jobs to do: greeting arrivals, making sure they have a drink, replenishing the food. These chores keep me circulating. I chat with people but I'm always on my way someplace else to do something. Basically, I'm fake mingling. I'm genuinely happy to see my friends and to show them a good time, but my brain has retreated to its quiet happy place and isn't up to anything complicated.

One of my readers wrote that she liked arriving at parties early, to get comfortable with the hosts and chat quietly with any other guests there before the hubbub began. But, she continued, "If I am able to make it through an entire party, my favorite part is usually the end, after most people have left. By then there aren't many people left, and those who are are winding down and a little more mellow. I've had some of my best party conversations during this time. It's also the time when the hosts are finally able to relax."

Small parties, like dinner parties, are nice. They're quieter, they allow time and leisure to connect with your dining companions.

Parties of ten to twenty people are a toss-up. You go and take your chances. They can be fun. But when they're not fun, small parties are hard to duck out on. You can't just make an appearance. People notice when you arrive and when you leave. You have to say your good-nights. This can be awkward if you're leaving before others think you should. (Awkward, but not your problem.)

Parties are part of the human experience, and they can be joyous. "You never know what is going to happen at a party, and it may be surprisingly fun," one introvert wrote. "Commit to staying for an hour, and see how you feel at the end of that time."

So even those of us who anticipate parties with fear and loathing keep going. We keep going because of intermittent reinforcement: We have fun just often enough to keep accepting party invitations. Sometimes we step in the door and become catatonic, sometimes we hang on for the white-knuckle ride, occasionally we throw up our hands and go *wheeee*!

But no matter what, we're rarely sorry when it's time to leave.

The Bathroom and Other Party Survival Skills

Every introvert alive knows the exquisite pleasure of stepping from the clamor of a party into the bathroom and closing the door.

You are alone. The din is muffled. Nobody is in your personal space. Nobody is talking. The bathroom offers quiet sanctuary, a moment to let your overstimulated brain relax, a moment of blissful solitude. You may or may not need to use the facilities, but you definitely needed to go to the bathroom.

Even good parties, where we're having fun, take a toll on our brains. If we have any hope of sticking them out, we need strategies and tactics. Like bathroom breaks. I suppose anyone who paid attention might assume I suffer from some sort of bladder disorder. But no, I just like the bathroom, where I can regroup and shake some of the words that have cluttered my brain out my ears.

Bookshelves also offer retreat at parties. Books are familiar friends, quiet friends. You can turn your back on the room for a few minutes to study your host's library, and it's as if the hubbub behind you barely exists. Sometimes I just pretend to look at books in order to turn my back and catch my breath. I know one woman who even brings a book into the bathroom during parties and reads for a few moments. A sort of introvert multitasking.

Pets, too, provide opportunity to ignore people for a minute. Getting down on the floor and spending a few minutes communing with quadrupeds can be so restful. They require nothing of us. Sometimes they even purr, if they're that kind of pet. If not, wagging is fun, too.

I still miss smoking, which I gave up several years ago. I loved stepping out for a smoke during parties. It's usually dark and quiet outside there, and you might become part of a small (and ever-shrinking) party subset: the smokers/pariahs. Obviously not a good reason to keep smoking, but those were good days for introverts.

Escape is one survival tactic, keeping busy is another. Some introverts like to be kitchen elves, finding glasses and wiping down counters and serving drinks. You meet a lot of people that way, but with purpose. Plus, at most parties, guests tend to gravitate toward the kitchen, so you can find yourself in the midst of the action without having to exert any mingling effort.

One introvert appointed himself unofficial photographer for his high school reunion. "I had a blast," he said. "I took more pictures than anyone else and they were generally the best shots of the night. Best of all, I didn't get bored and leave after thirty minutes, as I would have without the camera in front of me."

Another said that just wandering through a large party keeps her at a quiet remove. "I'm still around people but I'm not forced to try to engage in any conversation unless I want to. Or if there's a game, or music, or a video playing, you can plant yourself there for a while and watch."

One introvert planned an escape from a necessary party she knew would wear her out by arranging for an introverted friend to be her "phone-a-friend." "I got a nice break in the car, having an actual meaningful conversation before going back in the house for pointless chitchat with people I have nothing in common with," she said. And since it was an actual phone call, she didn't have to lie when she explained that the call had been from an old friend she hadn't spoken to in a long time.

Planting myself in one spot for stretches of time tends to be my main party strategy. I find comfortable spots that are both out of the way and in proximity to high traffic, so that everyone drifts by me at some point. It's like inertia mingling. I get a little small talk in, and then the minglers can mingle away and I can wait for the next one. I'm like an ocean sponge feeding on plankton. But better dressed.

No law says everyone must enjoy parties, and if you absolutely positively can't bear them, then the solution is to politely decline. Eventually people will stop inviting you and presumably you would be fine with that. But me—I'd get my feelings hurt if I were never invited to parties. I don't hate them, and I like the people who throw them. But I will assert my right to enjoy parties my own way, which means less time mingling and more time in the bathroom, if necessary. And it usually is.

Hell Is a Cocktail Party

What is it about chitchat that sucks the life force out of me? That's the big question. But first, a moment in defense of small talk:

Small talk is the WD-40 of society. It has a purpose, perhaps many purposes. A few niceties with a sales clerk, a little joshing with your dentist's receptionist, some light get-to-know-ya banter with a stranger at a party—it keeps the gears of society cranking smoothly, makes the world feel friendly, and protects our social muscles from atrophy.

It is good for us to push past our solitary nature to connect with other people, even casually. Being introverted does not and should not, I think, mean being isolated. Sure, we need to respect our need for solitude, but we must show equal respect to the benefits of connections. If that means leaving our comfort zone sometimes, so be it. Sometimes things we don't like are good for us. That's life.

Chitchat is the gateway to friendship, a necessary ritual before you may attempt more substantial conversation. You can't make friends if you don't talk to people, and jumping right into deep philosophical discussion can be off-putting. Or it can lead to a hasty burnout—a flare of conversational heat and then, well, um, okay . . . nice talkin' to you. Chitchat is where all human connections start in our world, so avoiding it altogether is neither an option nor a pleasant thought.

The problem is that more often than not, chitchat is an end unto itself. Especially in situations where you are expected to circulate. Like cocktail parties. Cocktail parties are, practically by definition, chitchat incubators. They're networking events at which extroverts can excel. But cocktail parties are particularly hard on introverts.

I have a terrible time with them. I stand frozen, drink in hand. The chatter flusters me. I can't flit around because my mind doesn't flit. I don't remember people's names, and realize even as they are speaking them that I won't remember. Yes, I have heard all the tricks to remember names, but I forget to do them. There's too much going on. It's a white-knuckle ride all the way. So I won't lie: I tend to avoid cocktail parties. If the point of a cocktail party is meeting people or networking, and I'm bad at that, then I see no point in attending.

But of course, cocktail parties are not the only places that sort of nattering is committed. Chitchat is all around us every day. It's a nonnegotiable requirement for life in a civilized society. And so we must know how to do at least a passable facsimile. And even find ways to enjoy it.

The most important thing I've come to understand about

small talk is that it isn't supposed to be fascinating. It's just supposed to be a friendly connection. Or, as one introvert put it, "It's not the content. It's the action." Try not to judge yourself or your conversational partner if you sound inane. It doesn't matter. If deep conversation is a doctoral dissertation, chitchat is a blog post. Maybe even a tweet. It's just a way of acknowledging another person's humanity. Letting it be what it is takes a lot of pressure off. Chitchat doesn't require full attention, it needn't have a point, and it doesn't matter if your little jokes go nowhere. Nobody cares, and all people will remember is if you smiled and gave responses that were at least in the ballpark.

Of course, sometimes small talk matters, like at office parties and networking events. Sometimes you have to decide if you are capable of making a good enough impression to justify making an appearance at these. If it sounds like the kind of thing that would put you into brain lock, why bother? If you absolutely must make an appearance, make an appearance. Nobody says you have to like it. Think of it as a job. Target a few people, shake a few hands, slap a back, and vamoose. Then, if you want to solidify any of the connections you made there, wow 'em with a follow-up email in that special introvert way you do.

Sometimes you can get out of producing palaver by just winding up an extrovert and letting him or her go. A couple of good questions to start the other person talking and you can just stand back and smile until you excuse yourself to go to the bathroom. And they'll remember you as absolutely charming.

If extended small talk is inevitable (hello, tableful of other friends of the friends of the bride), take control and aim for middle ground between profound conversation and trivial chatter.

Ask questions that might have compelling answers. Use your introvert radar to home in on an interesting aspect of that person and steer the conversation there. You might even learn something you don't know. What's it like in a tax accountant's office on April 14? What does the social studies teacher teach his high school students about the 1960s? Why was that a good location for a dry-cleaning shop? "Why" questions are good. They might not to lead to anything gripping, but at least the answer should have some substance.

Of course, asking questions can be perilous. If you inadvertently trigger a chatterbox, you can do one of two things: Plaster a polite smile on your face and retreat to a happy place in your head, or go to the bathroom. Talking a blue streak is rude, so don't worry about being impolite if you need to come up with an excuse to extricate yourself from the monologue. There's nothing impolite about escaping before your head explodes. (One introvert confessed that when he's trapped by a talker, he introduces his extroverted wife "and then walk away and know I won't even be missed." Mean. But kinda clever.)

Small talk at its best is entrée into more interesting conversation. At its worst, it's awkward non sequiturs and forced laughs. But the benefit of accepting your chitchat obligations at a party or other event—even if you have to duck into the bathroom for solitude after each bout—is that other people will be much less likely to pester you with "Are you having fun?" or "Are you okay?" They will see you fulfilling standard social obligations and be satisfied.

Fact 1: Some People Are Boring.
Fact 2: You Are Not Obligated to Listen to Them.

ntroverts sometimes are accused of finding people boring. I am not innocent of the charge. I am bored by boring people. I'm bored by long stories about people I don't know. I'm bored by babble. I'm especially bored by anyone whose idea of conversation is a monologue.

"It's like you have a sign on you that says, 'Tell me about it,'" my husband marveled after rescuing me from a young woman, a stranger, who had me pinned in a corner at a gallery opening and was filling me in on everything that had happened to her since second grade.

Because introverts are comfortable with silence, we're sitting ducks for chatterboxes. One of the perils of living as an introvert is being cornered by boring people.

Introverts tend to be excellent listeners. I'm certainly better at listening to chatter than producing it. I am bumfuzzled by people I see in cars, on streets, at the supermarket, nattering away on their cell phones. What do they find to talk about for so long and enthusiastically? My policy is: Say what you have to say and then stop talking. Sometimes I lose interest in what I'm saying halfway through a sentence and trail off, much to my husband's irritation. It's difficult for me to imagine producing an unbroken stream of words. I can hold up my end of a conversation and love lively discourse. But I'm amazed and astounded by people who can stretch an anecdote to twenty minutes, with digressions to god knows where, around the block a few times, downtown and uptown and crosstown before bringing it home—and then take a deep breath and start again. When a chatterbox like that starts in on me, I've lost the battle before it even starts. I go conversationally limp.

Being a good listener and having an ability to draw people out are skills necessary for a good writer. I just don't know how to put people back again when I'm done. When he's cornered by a talker, my husband has a way of staring into the distance and becoming nonresponsive until the chatterbox falls silent. But I do all the wrong things: I make eye contact, encouraging noises and murmur appropriate responses—even as I become increasingly desperate for the words to stop. For the love of god. Please.

One reason listening can be exhausting for introverts is that we pay attention. We listen hard. Words enter our ears and then go straight to our busy, whirring brains to be processed, considered, and analyzed. Since we take what we say seriously, we try to take what everyone else says seriously, too. But let's face it: Not everything everyone says matters. A lot of it is just empty air. Not everyone deserves our A-game.

Along with the words being spoken, we also often hear, in our busy heads, all the unspoken back stories, context, and motivations behind them. When a story drags on, I start analyzing why this person might be telling me this now. What is the subtext? The woman telling a long story of vacation derring-do wants me to admire her. The one talking about the novel she will write someday is trying to convince herself she really will. The guy whose stories all seem to lead to "I was so drunk . . ." is either boasting or crying for help. Maybe I'm right, maybe not, and certainly I'm not required to do anything with these assumptions. They just give me something to do while the chatter continues.

As a writer, I try to tell myself that people's stories provide fodder for my stories, but that only keeps me interested for the first four hundred fifty thousand words. Otherwise, if I can't extricate myself, I amuse myself by looking for stories behind the stories. And if that doesn't work, I just retreat to the quiet place in my head and go into a sort of listening Zen, letting the words swirl around me. If I can give myself permission to not take every word seriously and mentally remove myself from the monologue to a quieter place, I can sit for quite a while before I feel like my head will explode. Then, off to the bathroom for quiet time.

Why listen at all, you ask? No particular reason; if you can recognize and dodge the yammerheads, then more power to you. "This may sound bad but I can usually tell within a couple of minutes if someone will interest me enough to make it worthwhile for me to have a conversation with them," one introvert admitted. "I'm sure I'm not always right, but I think I'm probably right enough of the time." Of course this introvert concedes, this tactic also means you might miss out on genuinely interesting people. It's up to us to figure out when to take the risk.

We all get trapped from time to time. Certainly our stay-put party tactic can be a liability in this case, especially if we settle in someplace where we can be backed up against a wall. Sometimes I genuinely like the chatterbox and want to be nice for as long as I can bear it. Sometimes there's no escape. You know: the dreaded airplane seatmate chatterbox. In those cases, I have learned to go to the happy place in my head. As long as I manage to maintain an appropriate facial expression, then I can let the words just skitter along the surface of my brain.

This is, however, a newly acquired skill. I used to listen, and listen hard, no matter who was talking. But now that I understand the toll that takes on me (and my desire to leave the house), I allow myself to check out sometimes, letting the talkers talk without expending real listening energy. I doubt they even notice.

Saying Yes When You Want to Say No (and Vice Versa)

Some researchers think extroverts are happier than introverts because social situations make everyone happy. Extroverts seek out more social situations, therefore they are happier.

We have already ascertained that happiness may not be one-size-fits-all, so this theory is flawed from the get-go. But we can also spin it according to your definition of social situations. For introverts, quantity does not make up for quality, and sometimes (often) happiness is a quiet room alone.

But although it's true that we get cranky after too much interaction, many of us also get gloomy after too much time alone. The trick is learning to discern when we need solitude, when we need interaction. Sometimes, even if my gut inclination is to hole up, I approach socializing like I do broccoli. It's good for me even when I'm not one hundred percent enthusiastic about it. (Although I like socializing more than I do broccoli. Usually. Sometimes.) So I weigh every invitation I receive carefully.

Some invitations are no-brainers. They either sound like so much fun I don't want to miss them, or they sound like such hell I can't imagine why anyone would invite me. But others put me squarely on the fence and I can talk myself into them as easily as I can talk myself out of them. I don't always want to go with my default, staying home, just because it's a lot easier. That's when I ask myself a series of questions that will lead me to a decision.

Is the invitation from someone I genuinely care about? If this person dropped out of my life forever, would that make the slightest difference to my happiness or well-being?

If this is someone important to me, does he or she need my presence for this event? (I believe that friends go to friends' parties to offer moral support, even if we don't stay the whole time.) Would this important person's feelings be genuinely hurt if I didn't show up? Good enough reason to go, in many cases. Especially if it's (a) a special occasion or (b) someone from whom I don't get a zillion invitations.

I ask myself if the invitation is to something my husband cares about attending. Does he need my presence? Is this something I want to do as a gesture of love and solidarity? My husband and I have a rule that we are not required to attend each others' events, but we also have the right to say, "This one, I really want you to come to." As long as he lets me off the hook for some events, I'll bite the bullet on others. And vice versa.

Is the invitation from someone I hope to nurture from casual friend to intimate? That requires putting in the time, even when I don't feel like it. These invitations get priority, unless they're to something that sounds like absolute hell. And even then, I think about it. If nothing else, it might show me a new side of a potential new friend.

Is this something I'm likely to enjoy once I get myself out there? Or is it something that I only *think* I should enjoy because everyone tells me I should? Introverts are not immune to FOMO—fear of missing out. Do you suffer FOMO over every invitation? Then you need to set that fear aside and consider the event in a different light. But if FOMO is rare for you, then take it seriously. After all, if you go and the event isn't any fun, you can leave. But if you miss it, you miss it forever. So consider whether it's a once-in-a-lifetime opportunity, something you might regret tomorrow morning if you blow it off today. Some things are worth doing just to be able to say you've done them. Or at least that's the way I feel about it. I went to my college graduation. Wore the cap and gown, the whole shebang. Even though I was in my forties. It mattered to me.

If you genuinely don't care about missing out on something, then just go with that. I'm not really one to recommend missing once-in-a-lifetime events, but if the senior prom, for example, really sounds like torture, who cares how many people say it's magical? Invent your own way to celebrate that night, something that feels significant to you. You probably have one or two friends who don't want to go to prom, either. Invite them.

If you have decided that an invitation is not for you, remember that saying no to invitations sometimes can be a sort of kindness. I had a friend who at first hurt my feelings when he declined my invitations. But then I realized how liberating that was. It meant I was free to say no, too. Your willingness to say no gives your friends permission to do the same, and they might be relieved. The worst thing to do is say yes to stuff and then back out at the last minute. Nobody likes a backer-outer. Now and then, sure. Everybody has to bail at the last minute sometimes. But doing it frequently is rude and only means that you need to learn to say no.

Saying no takes practice. You can always make up an excuse, as long as you're not at risk of getting caught in the lie. I'm not a big advocate of that. Maybe because I'm not a great liar. Another tactic is to substitute an introvert-friendly invitation: "Thanks so much, I'm going to pass on the party, but I would love to get together for lunch." And there's always the breezy, "Thanks, but I'm going to have to miss this one."

You don't actually have to explain why you are declining an invitation, and hopefully the person extending it knows it would be rude to press for an explanation. But if you are pressed, you can be truthful ("I'm not big on big parties" or "I've been looking forward to a quiet weekend") or you can make something up. An introverted friend and I laughed to learn that we had both independently concluded that "diarrhea" is the best excuse/lie when you need something ironclad. People would assume that nobody would lie about something that embarrassing, and they're not going to want any details. (I have never actually used this excuse, but I keep it in mind for emergencies.)

But before you say no, ask yourself one last question: Have I been in a hermit stretch? Is it time to just get out and soak in some stimulation? Here's where you might need to say yes even if part of you thinks the whole thing sounds like a hassle. Sometimes, when I've been a hermit for a while, inertia sets in. Then, even if something sounds fun, I'm likely to decide it's too much trouble. Or blow it off at the last minute. Then I'm very likely to regret the decision. Sometimes I need to drag my ass out whether I think I want to or not.

As much as we all want to assert our right to be loners, introverts, and quiet homebodies, people do need people. And so at the same time as we learn to say no even when we feel pressured to say yes, we also should learn to say yes sometimes when part of us is saying no. As long as we do it for our own good reasons and not simply to please others, getting out there can be good for us.

So can staying home.

Extroversion in a Bottle

There probably isn't an introvert alive who hasn't tried the one-more-margarita route to extroversion. Alcohol lowers inhibitions, and many of us need a little bit of that to plunge into a party. A little drinkie to take the edge off isn't a bad thing, if you're a little-drinkie kind of person. But too many little drinkies in your quest to be an extrovert party person can backfire.

Even if you don't have an actual drinking problem, alcohol can be a crutch to help you push through a party when you'd rather go home. Anesthetic, perhaps. "I want to be with my friends and they get frustrated when I bail early so I figure, why not drink a lot and stay?" wrote an introverted college student.

At best, drinking away your introversion doesn't work. "[E]ven when I'm drunk, I'm still totally introverted!" the student continued. "My friends will want to go from party to party and I want to go back to my room!"

At worst, it can turn you into someone you don't like and

don't want to be. A drink or two over my line and I am guaranteed intense middle-of-the-night regrets. I'm unlikely to do anything genuinely risky or extreme under the influence. I do, however, live in general with a robust horror of looking foolish, and drinking is often a direct route to looking foolish. Back home after a drinkie or two too many, fear and shame will kick in as the room spins and I review the evening. That too-boisterous moment. That too-loud laugh. That know-it-all contribution to a conversation. All sorts of behavior that makes me cringe. It's not me. It's drunken me.

Why didn't I stop myself? Because with alcohol we reach a point where even if we know we're being boorish, we just don't care. At that moment, that is. Later, however, at home, in the dark, we might care very deeply. I've had some whoppers of middle of the night self-loathing fests after too much booze. (As you probably know, alcohol interferes with sleep, so after too many drinks I'm pretty much guaranteed to wake an hour or two after falling asleep. And, as you also know, everything always seems a whole lot worse in the middle of the night.)

Happily, this rarely happens anymore. I'm old enough to know better, which is usually what happens over time to anyone without a bona fide drinking problem. You live, you learn, you recognize when you're about to go one drink over the line. Sometimes you know you're going a drink over the line and do it anyway, just for the helluvit. That can be fun sometimes. Not often, though. Not to me.

We don't have research on introverts and drinking, but we do know that shy people are usually not big drinkers. They'll have a drink or two to get through a party, though nothing much, compared to other people. Shy people aren't big risk takers. They don't want to drink and drive; they don't want to do anything dumb or silly. This can generalize to a degree to introverts. We tend not to be impulsive and are likely to think it through before we have one more.

And introverts who are accustomed to sitting and watching the party have witnessed all sorts of sloppy behavior out of extroverts who don't give a damn. While I sometimes admire the extrovert's spirit of not giving a damn, the attitude is difficult to adopt. I'm just too self-conscious. Even if my behavior barely registers on the dumb-ass meter for other people, my tolerance for my own silly behavior is very low.

But at the same time, introverts also are often sensitive to the wants and needs of the people around us, and this makes us vulnerable to peer pressure. Extroversion in a bottle is probably more common among college kids at what one introverted student called "that awkward age, where parties are the focus." College kids face a lot of pressure to stick around, hang with the crowd, have another, and another. *Beer bong! Fuzzy Nipples! Jägermeister!* Even adults, though, can often be swayed by a congenial host wielding a wine bottle.

You're gonna drink too much sometimes. Most of us do. But it can't hurt, before the next drink, to ask yourself if you're having another because you really want to go home. Then make your decision. Maybe you just need to find a nice introvert corner of the party for some downtime, to refresh your head. Taking breathers from the action can be almost as rejuvenating as another drink. If that doesn't work, would it be so terrible if you went home? Or refused the next drink? Or pretended a glass of water was vodka?

Whatever it takes. Resisting peer pressure is a muscle you have to exercise, at your own pace, but it starts with knowing your own mind, which is better done with a clear head.

Alcohol might make you behave more extroverted at a party. But before you down that drink too many, look around at other people who are already drunk. Is that the extrovert you want to be?

Postscript: Speaking of parties and vices, I quit smoking cigarettes three years ago and still miss them at parties, when a smoke gives you an excuse to duck outside. I believe my introversion prolonged my habit because I smoked at parties long after I stopped smoking most other places. Now I party-smoke vicariously through my husband's habit, following him outside to the smoking section. When he quits, we might have to just hang outside with the smokers like some kind of smoker groupies.

There Must Be Fifty Ways to Leave a Party

Having a party escape hatch is crucial for introverts. Knowing we can leave makes showing up a lot easier. But deciding ahead of time that you're going to leave is not the same thing as actually opening the door and leaving, which can be harder than it sounds. When they see you trying to leave, people will want you to believe one of two things: Either (1) you are going to miss *the best party ever* or (2) your absence will cause the entire party to collapse in gloom.

Neither of these is true. In fact, once the door closes behind you, most people will forget you were even there. No offense, but you know it's true.

In a post titled "An Introvert's Guide to Spontaneous Departures" on her blog *Copylicious*, Kelly Parkinson offered some particularly good advice: "Look like you are having *the time of your life* as you say goodbye," she wrote. "Never leave a party early looking tired. It's a common introvert mistake. You want everyone to secretly suspect you're going to another party, so they don't feel sorry for you."

Pretending you have someplace to go is an excellent way to avoid pity or pressure. Yeah, yeah, it's all part of the (Extrovert) Man holding down the introvert. But what's most important here? Getting out of the party.

Sometimes you don't even have to say good-bye. My husband and I once went very reluctantly to a baby shower (does anybody really enjoy those?), but arrived at the party to find that mommy had gone into labor early, and she and daddy were at the hospital. My husband and I didn't know a soul in the room. So we started looking at the . . . art . . . hanging . . . on . . . the . . . walls . . . until we were by the front door and, zoom, outta there. High-fiving occurred. Now "Let's look at the art" is one of our code phrases for "Let's get the hell out of here."

We have a few codes like that, mostly developed in the party trenches. One favorite was a spontaneous expression after several hours at a Mardi Gras party. It was a great party and we'd eaten, drunk, laughed, chatted, watched a parade, wore beads. But after a few hours (I got through it with frequent visits to the quiet apartment balcony), my husband sidled up to me and muttered, "I'm sick of wearing these beads." When I finished laughing at the sheer perfection of the expression, we left. We've used the phrase many times since.

At big parties, it's easy to be the disappearing guest. One minute you're there, the next you're gone. Thanking your host is always polite, of course, but it's easily done the next day. Your host is probably too busy and distracted to notice that you're gone, anyway. And if you do it right, you can slip out before anyone else notices and lays the "You're not leaving already?" guilt trip on you. You can pretend you're just . . . stepping . . . out . . . for . . . a . . . little . . . air . . .

Of course, if you go to a party with an extrovert, prying that person out early can be difficult and isn't really fair. That's why you should bring your own wheels (or cab fare) whenever possible. You probably won't break your friend's heart by leaving. "By the time you leave, your extrovert friend will have found a new and shiny friend," wrote Parkinson.

So don't worry about it. Slip out the back, or put on a big smile and parade out, waving and air-kissing. Just leave when it's time to leave, however you can do it. Because—and this is the take-home message—leaving parties when you're ready makes going to them a lot more fun.

Life Through Introvert Eyes

You see a couple sitting in a restaurant over Sunday brunch. Each has a newspaper and they are reading as they eat.

This is like an introvert/extrovert Rorschach test.

As an introvert, you probably think: Ah, how nice. This couple is starting their Sunday together with coffee and the newspaper. I'd love to be in a relationship that comfortable and relaxed.

Whereas an extrovert might think: How tragic! This couple is ignoring each other! I wouldn't want to be in a relationship that cold and unconnected!

This situation came up on the Facebook status of an extremely extroverted friend (judging by the number of party pictures she posts), who spotted a couple at breakfast, each absorbed in an e-reader. My friend saw it as an ominous sign that technology is destroying human connections, and posted something to that effect in her status line. I suggested that perhaps the couple was reading the Sunday paper, via new technology, over breakfast.

After all, reading the Sunday paper together is a treasured ritual for many people (including me and my husband).

No matter, my friend said. It's rude.

Well. Hmm. Okay. If that's the way you see it. Some of us see it entirely differently.

"I usually look around [restaurants], gaping at all the people talking to each other and think 'don't they see each other all the time, why are they talking so much?!?'" one introvert commented.

I understand that. I feel the same way about people on the streets or highways, in line at the supermarket, or in department store dressing rooms, chattering away on cell phones. When I can hear their conversations, they mostly seem banal. That's my perception, anyway. And perception is everything.

Take the woman who said her ex-husband used the fact that she had few friends as proof that she was a loser. Sure, seen one way, someone with just a handful of friends is to be pitied, maybe even scorned as somehow unlikable. But seen the introvert way, someone with a small number of friends has more time and attention for each. Perhaps those friendships have more depth. Perhaps. Or maybe not. Maybe we're all just different.

I'm not particularly comfortable being friends with people who have bajillions of friends—my perception is that I'm lost in a crowd. I prefer feeling special. Chosen. That's perception, too, because it's entirely possible that extroverts with lots of friends have a different capacity for caring about people—perhaps even in their blizzard of friends they manage to consider each and every one of us a special snowflake. Some extroverts can shine their light on you in such a way that you actually feel like a standout. Sometimes that's not genuine, but other times it is. We cannot know the ways of the extrovert heart. We only know the behaviors.

But in some very essential ways, introverts and extroverts see things differently. The small talk that binds the world together is music to extroverts' ears but a racket to introverts'. A big party might look like a thousand new friends to an extrovert, but like a waste of time (at best) to an introvert. The ring of a telephone might sound like an opportunity to an extrovert, but like an interruption to an introvert. An evening without plans is bliss to introverts but social failure to extroverts. Introverts might consider a cell phone a ball and chain, but it's a lifeline for extroverts. Team-building exercises look like arcane torture to introverts, but they look like team-building exercises to extroverts. (I do, of course, speak broadly here. Not all parties look like hell to introverts, nor do all quiet evenings feel like social failure to extroverts.)

I have an intellectual understanding of extroverts' perceptions of the world and I'm well trained in the behaviors. But I'm stymied when I try to actually *feel* them, to put myself in extroverts' brains. I can say "Oh goody" when the phone rings, but my heart isn't in it. My attempts to mingle with strangers when I'm not feeling it can be awkward and weird. And while I can go through the motions of cocktail party talk, I find it no more nourishing than the canapés.

Still, the more I start trying to see the world through extrovert eyes, the more at ease I am with extrovert ways. They mean no harm. They just want us to have fun the way they see it. So the next time you find yourself rankled by an extrovert's behavior, maybe try putting on extrovert goggles and see how the situation looks through them.

"It'll Be Fun!" They Say, But We Beg to Differ

L et's just start with the disclaimer: You might like the activities I'm going to discuss. You are free to disagree with me.

You also will probably have other things to add to the list. Introversion is only one aspect of who we are. We have a lot in common, but we're not carbon copies.

Still, we can probably agree on a few things that extroverts consider super-duper fun but that make us want to hide in a closet. In an extroverted world, we frequently must justify our reluctance to participate in activities that make extroverts giddy with delight. They can hardly believe that the kind of fun that makes them tingle either leaves us cold or fills us with horror. They try to assure us that really, if we just get over ourselves and try, we'll have a grand time.

Sometimes we allow ourselves to be persuaded. Usually, at best, it's okay. We rarely enjoy it as much as they insist we will. No matter how much I open my mind when trying something that doesn't sound like fun, I don't have fun. For example, I never thought I would enjoy a roller coaster. Finally, one day, when I was in my mid-twenties, a friend persuaded me to try a roller coaster. I figured I should try everything once. I tried two that day, actually. Just to be a good sport, and to be extra sure. Guess what? I didn't enjoy either one and never did it again.

Some other things I'd rather not, thanks:

Karaoke: I don't mind watching other people do it, but step up there myself? Uh-uh. That's for exhibitionists. I performed in theatrical productions as a kid and enjoyed that, but karaoke is more intimate. Plus you have to sit down among your audience when you're done. People might have gotten the wrong impression and think you'd like to chat. Sometimes even watching karaoke makes me uncomfortable. I hate seeing people look foolish. I appreciate the courage and spirit, I really do, but also get embarrassed for them sometimes.

Audience participation: Nothing fills me with more terror than being stuck in a seat near the front when a performer starts scanning the audience for a volunteer. I try to emit death rays to protect myself. The thought of being dragged up on stage to wing it in front of an audience, when anything can happen, is too terrible to contemplate. You might be the stooge. You might feel obligated to try witty banter. I can't even come up with good one-liners with the supermarket checker, I'd probably just babble non sequiturs onstage. Maybe that doesn't matter, but it also doesn't sound like fun.

"I still have nightmares about the time in seventh grade when I was 'chosen' to be serenaded onstage by a group of singers from

Spain," said one introvert. "I'm happy to be an audience member, but don't make me participate. Just don't."

Costume parties: I don't like being around adults in costume because they tend to lose their inhibitions and I'm a big fan of inhibitions. I don't want people all up in my face, acting out their costumes. Costumes require a response from their audience. It's just more audience participation. Once again, in the abstract, I admire and respect the creativity of a good costume. In the real world, it's a person wearing something silly and I don't know what to do with that. I just don't care. And I mean that in the nicest way. Go. Have fun. I'll sit it out. And I'll enjoy looking at the photos tomorrow.

Skinny-dipping: Maybe alone. Or alone with a significant other. Or even with very close friends. But when someone says, "Hey gang, let's go skinny-dipping!" and it inspires whoops of joy from the crowd, I'm out. Could anything be more extroverted than taking off all your clothes in front of friends and acquaintances?

Practical jokes: Hahaha. Very funny. Now go away and leave me alone. I can't even watch shows like *Punk'd* and *Candid Camera*, and the idea of getting into a practical joke war gives me hives. Having a joke played on you is not just attention, it's negative attention. Yeah, yeah, they're not laughing at me, they're laughing with me. But what if I'm not laughing? And I'm probably not.

I'm sure there are things introverts do that extroverts don't enjoy. I recall once, on a trip out of the country, inviting a couple of my travel companions to go to an art museum with me. "No, thanks," one said. "We're not museum people. We'd rather be outside, where *life* is."

So I went by myself and spent a happy couple of hours at the museum, surrounded by other presumably dead people.

I'm always a little shocked to be reminded that not everyone enjoys museums. I shouldn't be. There's nothing wrong with those people, just as there's nothing wrong with those of us who don't karaoke.

Don't let anyone shame you into pretending you find something fun. At the same time, let them have their fun without judging. There's room in the world for karaoke people and museum people.

Fun, Introvert Style

Fun for introverts doesn't look like fun to extroverts because it almost never involves throwing our hands in the air and going "*Whoooo!*" It's rarely loud and it might not even require smiling. Fun for introverts often entails a look of concentration.

Like our concept of happiness, society's concept of fun has been claimed by extroverts. Fun is a Mountain Dew commercial. Those commercials for fancy coffee that show a woman sipping coffee by a rain-spattered window? Nice and introvertish, but not "fun" as we know it.

Yeah, well, it's time for introverts to reclaim fun.

Introvert fun is quiet, contemplative, and often experienced in solitude. It frequently relates to our environment. A peaceful place is conducive to our kind of fun. So is a slowed pace. And time. We like quiet sports that let us get into our thoughts, sports that can be enjoyed alone or with other like-minded quiet types: hiking, biking, kayaking, mountain climbing. We like being near water. We like swimming. "At my first lesson, my teacher cautioned me that swimming was a solitary sport—as if that were a drawback—and all I thought was 'Great!' " one introvert said.

We like walking—in the woods, around the neighborhood, with a dog or without, with music or without. We don't mind walking with a friend now and then, as a way to have a nice visit. We like yoga and meditation.

We like reading. "Sometimes I even send the dog to 'camp' for a weekend so I can read all day," said one introvert.

We like coffee shops, either for a cozy visit with friends or as a place to recharge. "After spending two or three hours in a coffee shop reading, I feel relaxed and completely restored," said another introvert.

We like a long lunch with a good friend, or small dinner parties involving wine and conversation. We like long, deep, self-absorbed, self-analytical, navel-gazing conversations with a close friend. A similarly disposed friend and I once took a weekend trip together and by the end of it, our jaws actually ached from so much talking. It was twenty-two hours of deep, intimate soul baring. It was great.

We like theaters, where we may sit quietly and nourish our brains. I'm not really a film buff, but I love sitting in the dark and being transported. Going to movies alone is deliciously indulgent. Going alone during the day is so much fun it's practically wicked.

We like looking out of windows, watching the passing scene, whether we're standing still or on the move. I adore road trips, alone or with my excellent husband, who is capable of long stretches of silence. The motion and changing view sends my thoughts down all sorts of interesting paths. And, one introvert mused, "drive the same route a few times and you begin to notice details that you previously missed."

We like getting up early or staying up late to have the house to ourselves. One introvert likes to "sleep in," but "I don't usually sleep when I stay in bed late. I like to just stay there and think or daydream."

We like knitting, sewing, drawing, writing. We enjoy the concentration these require, and the creative outlet. We like making PowerPoint presentations—or at least one of us does. "I find I really get caught up in this and enjoy making it look good," said one introvert.

"I also like to refinish furniture," said another. "I find it soothing. Often, my spouse will be twenty feet away, working on some airbrush project. We'll work for hours without speaking."

We like art galleries and museums. We like parks, where we can walk or sit and watch. We like days with nothing on our schedule, and evenings alone watching six consecutive episodes of our favorite show. A night at home alone with the TV might not sound like fun to some people. And sure, we don't mind the right kind of company for a night like that. But we don't need company, and often we don't want it.

"My favorite fun things are totally different experiences when I do them alone and when I do them with another person," said one introvert. "Alone is a more spiritual adventure to me."

"Spiritual fun" sounds practically like an oxymoron. That's because we've allowed the Mountain Dew people to take possession of the word "fun." But it's time to stake our claim to it, by identifying and owning the activities that give us genuine pleasure and refusing to let anyone tell us we don't know how to have fun.

Friends, "Friends," Acquaintances, and Why Bother?

What is a friend? We probably all have our own definitions. For me, it's someone I don't feel alone with. Who doesn't bore me. Whose life I connect with and who takes reciprocal interest in my life. It's someone I feel comfortable turning to when I need to be talked off the ledge, and for whom I am glad to return the favor.

Just a few people in my life fit that bill.

We all know how lonely we can get in a crowd, even a party full of people we know. Loneliness is not about being physically alone, but about whether you feel emotionally or intellectually connected. Flighty friendships don't fill introverts' need for connection, and quantity doesn't make up for quality.

In 1992, anthropologist Robin Dunbar did some anthropological hocus-pocus and came up with "Dunbar's number" of 150, which is widely accepted as the number of relationships we are cognitively capable of keeping straight. I probably have a network of that many people in my life. I certainly wouldn't call them all friends, though. And even fewer of them would fit the label true friend.

I don't fling the word "friend" around freely. Some people are more appropriately called acquaintances, colleagues, or online friends, an entirely new category for a modern world. Some of the people with whom I pal around on Facebook are real-world friends, the others I think of as "friends." They are very different, but even on Facebook I'm not promiscuous about accepting "friend" requests.

One study concluded that the ideal number of Facebook "friends"—enough so you don't seem pathetic, not so many that you seem needy—is 302. Research also shows that no matter how many Facebook "friends" we have, we actually interact with only about five to ten percent of them. I've never done the math on my "friends," but ten percent sounds right. Those are the keepers. And maybe a few people I just find generally interesting. The rest? Perfectly nice people, I'm sure, but not friends. Hardly even "friends."

At times, taking friendship so seriously is a drawback. If real friends are not close by, or if they are for some reason unavailable, introverts can get lonely. At one point, a number of my friends moved away, to new cities. I had a long, lonely stretch when that happened. Making friends isn't always easy for introverts because we are reserved and it takes time for a connection to strengthen into a genuine bond.

I don't suggest that true friendship is different for extroverts, but superficial relationships may be more satisfying for them than they are for us, a better placeholder when true friends are out-of-pocket. When I feel a need to be with people (we all do, or possibly should) I sometimes have to weigh whether the need for connection outweighs the exhausting aspect of socializing with acquaintances or colleagues.

Perhaps there should be another level, a name for people who are a step up from acquaintances but not the person to call during a personal crisis. People who are, perhaps, in the transitional phase between acquaintances and friends, who with more time and conversation might one day be full-fledged friends. These actually are valuable individuals to have in your life and I try to keep an eye out for them. It can be awkward the first time you, for example, extend a first after-hours invitation to a coworker you've always enjoyed being around, but it can be worth a shot. It never hurts to have potential friends in the pipeline.

There is a precarious point for introverts in nascent friendships. Once we start investing in a friendship, we start weighing what we get back. It's a make-or-break time. And for introverts, the investment can feel costly in terms of energy expended. It's the point when we start asking, "why bother?"—a legitimate question, as long as it's treated as a question rather than a blow off. Is this person willing to see you, and fun to be with, one-on-one? Does the conversation flow? Is it satisfying? Do you feel energized or depleted after time with this person? I love friendships where the conversation is so interesting, you can't end it even when the visit is supposed to be over. You stand in doorways, you sit in stopped cars, you stand on street corners, finishing up conversations that potentially have no end. Sure, those long conversations are exhausting, but they give my brain so much new fodder, they remain satisfying long after the talking is done.

Anyone who doesn't meet these criteria will be relegated to one of my friendly-but-not-friend lists: acquaintance, colleague, or "friend." These are people I enjoy in a specific context but who don't get access to anything behind the curtain of my dog and pony show.

Sometimes another person clearly would like to be my friend, but I just don't feel it. I feel a little bad when that happens, but if I know the investment won't pay off for me, I trust my instincts and keep my boundaries intact. These are usually perfectly fine people and I wish them well. But there's nothing wrong with being discerning and saving your energy for people who give energy back to you.

The Online Extrovert

n many ways, the Internet is a godsend for introverts. What scientists call computer-mediated communication (CMC)—texting, blogging, Facebook—gives us control of our airspace and time to think before we respond, making it an ideal medium for letting us get our thoughts out. We don't have to try to wedge ourselves into conversations, we can just chime in anytime and take as long as it takes to say what we have to say.

"[W]ritten communication allows me to take the time to gather my thoughts and write something meaningful, rather than the idle chatter that seems to come out in most spoken conversations," one introvert commented.

I fell in love with email immediately. I always have one or two email buddies with whom I email daily, a stream of updates, one-liners, shared links, and occasional deep conversations. I've spilled a lot of guts in email over the years. And I had to learn a lesson about not fighting with friends via email. (It escalates far too quickly without body language and the warmth of a real person in front of you.) I also conduct most of my business via email.

With Facebook, my online social life expanded tremendously. Some introverts consider Facebook just another form of mindless chatter, but I'm a big fan. For me, alone in my home office, Facebook is like having colleagues in nearby cubicles. We swap one-liners, do a little shoptalk, share interesting articles and recipes, commiserate, and cheer each other on. I play Scrabble. In fact, acquaintances have matured into friends in the course of playing online games— this is a great low-stress way for introverts to make new friends. It's slow and steady and you get to know each other with no more pressure than landing a triple word score.

And on the Internet I can easily ignore anyone who seems a waste of time. Sometimes Facebook feels like a party where I can comfortably sit on the sidelines and watch without anyone tugging at my arm. (Happily, we've moved past those irritating FB "pokes.") And I don't accept every friend request that comes my way. I have a decent number of Facebook friends, but I don't need everyone. I'm almost as choosy about Facebook friends as I am real friends. People who mock Facebook make much of the triviality and narcissism of status lines. The way I see it, if the status lines of your friends are relentlessly boring and self-centered, you need more interesting friends.

The doomsday scenario about computer-mediated communication is that people will use it to replace face-to-face interaction. Nah. We'll always need face-to-face interaction. If anything, CMC will replace the telephone. Remember, in 2008 a Nielsen survey found that people were sending more texts with their mobile phones than making phone calls. To which I say: Right on, right on. If CMC replaces the telephone, introverts won't miss it a bit.

Like many introverts, I love texting for its efficiency. When I want to say "Meet me here" or "Pick up milk," I'd much rather do it via text than telephone. For some reason people think it's rude if you call, say what you need to say, and immediately hang up. But with text, nobody cares. Introverts love CMC not because we fear people or any such hogwash. We like it because it suits our style.

And with the exception perhaps of shy people, who may feel emboldened online, we generally are the same people we are offline, online. Despite paranoid suspicions about people putting up false fronts on social networking sites, researchers have found that people are pretty consistent online and off.

In an online forum for introverts, one person wrote about joining Facebook as a way to get to know new coworkers, all of whom were on it. But, "I grew bored with it very quickly and stopped logging in for a long time. I finally canned it last year and don't miss it in the slightest."

What you are is what you are.

My emails tend to be either terse and efficient communications or long and thoughtful conversations. Just like my conversations in the real world. Like in the real world, introverts tend toward frugality with words online. We don't like pointless yammering any more online than we do off. I obviously have a higher tolerance for it than the introvert who got bored on Facebook, but I do hide people who seem like empty noise.

And if you're like me and enjoy Facebook (or blogging, or Tumblr), you're probably pretty proficient at it. We're good at finding and sharing interesting articles and links because we like quietly poking around online. I'm quite sure that my blog about introversion gets a lot of readers because introverts enjoy sitting in front of their computers. We find lots of good stuff and are happy to pass it around. And sharing links or thoughtful status lines is a great way to get interesting conversations started. Toss it out there, see who bites.

Twitter also can suit an introvert's style. We're good at saying things in as few words possible, so the 140-character limit is fine for us. Twitter is, one introvert posted in an online discussion, "great for minimal cutting sarcastic commenting. :)"

Nevertheless, as much as I like CMC, by the end of a workday, all the voices online start giving me the same kind of tired head I get at a party or after a stretch of face-to-face social engagements. Again, we are who we are. Sometimes I find myself getting annoyed when people comment on my status lines, which is silly. If you're going to be an exhibitionist, you have to expect people to look. That's when I know it's time to shut down the dog and pony show.

Sometimes just shutting down for the night is enough; sometimes I need a weekend off. When I'm traveling and have little time to goof around online, I have that same feeling of surprised relief as when a noise I hadn't been consciously aware of suddenly goes quiet.

And sometimes I feel a strong need to shut off CMC and get out among flesh and blood. I start feeling dry and dusty and tired of tiny faces in squares. I need more oomph to my interactions. Then I make a date, or maybe two or three.

It's important for introverts to remain ever alert and sensitive to when we're letting CMC dominate our social lives out of sheer inertia. It's not that we prefer online interaction, but it's so much easier than going out. Staying home is the default, and even easier to default to when we don't have to feel isolated if we don't want to. So keep vigilant and know your own warning signs that you're living in your computer too much.

Computer-mediated communication can be fun and fulfilling. But like all other forms of communication, only up to a point.

The Happy Noise of Extroversion

A self-identified extrovert recently asked me why introverts are drawn to extroverts, especially when extroverts might make them do horrible things like go to parties. She was kidding, sort of, but the question is good. And even now, my answer is that there is no easy answer. Relationships are a complicated stew, each one different.

Some of us surround ourselves with extroverts who, one introvert pointed out, are great for those of us who like to sit back and watch the fun. "Extroverts are by far the most fun to watch," he said. And some extroverts are drawn to introverts. "It's more of a challenge to get them to open up," one wrote in an online forum. "Also, once they feel like they can open up to you, they are crazy, and a lot of fun most of the time."

As for extroverts—they are great fun when you crave a little razzle-dazzle in your life. When you're feeling up to it, an extrovert is a happy noise. Extroverts are game. They're always up for it, whatever it is, in a way that introverts may not be. Friendship with extroverts means happyfungoodtimes with lots of people, and that's cool. Actually, it can be more than cool. It can be good for us. "When I was a kid, my best friend was an extrovert. Other friends were, too," said one introvert. "I guess, even at a young age, I knew that if someone didn't get me out of the house, I'd become a cave dweller."

It can be fun to coast along on extrovert energy, said another introvert, who married an extrovert and admires her social agility. As long as nobody gets hurt, there's nothing wrong with riding extroverts' coattails and letting them do the heavy lifting socially while you enjoy the scene. One introvert pointed out that some of his closest friends are extroverts—and he never would have imagined being friends with them until they somehow became friends.

But even introverts who are drawn to extroverts might find them exhausting. And it's not always easy to get extroverts to understand that you're not being a spoilsport but actually need home-alone time. "I have found that maintaining friendships, especially those with extroverts, can be difficult," an introvert wrote. "I don't mind talking on the phone, meeting them for lunch, or listening to my friend's problems, but these things seem to drag on far beyond my capacity. Often, I find myself drained for the rest of the day."

We might find ourselves keeping our friendships with extreme extroverts at a casual level. Among other reasons, it can be hard for an introvert to solidify a friendship that exists only in a crowd. Extroverts who don't understand that my friendship also requires one-on-one time never graduate from acquaintance (or even close acquaintance) to what I consider a friend.

Other introverts seem to surround themselves with extroverts unintentionally and then feel like oddballs. Introverts living among extroverts might want to search their psyches to make sure they are not confusing introversion with shyness. Is it possible you love being around people but are fearful? You can overcome shyness if you choose. That's not necessary if you find that hanging with extroverts fulfills your social needs, but if you often find yourself feeling trapped and lonely in a noisy crowd, perhaps you are not drawn into relationships with extroverts as much as you drift into them.

Consider a woman who wrote to advice columnist Carolyn Hax because she kept finding herself in relationships with charming cads, all of whom had pursued her. Hax responded, "You are, I'm guessing, an introvert, hanging back and letting people choose you. Charm and charisma are a lot of fun, and they're like a tonic for introverts—they draw you out, engage you, spare you from having to start or sustain conversations . . ."

Introverts also can be attractive to extroverts, especially "center of attention types," as one introvert describes them. For one thing, we listen well, which is a drug for extroverts with a lot to say. Plus, we never compete for attention in social situations. This can be great for our extroverted friends, who gather fuel from attention.

Admittedly, this can be a drawback for us at times. I sometimes struggle to get my say when I'm in a social situation with extroverts. I've had many conversations hijacked by extroverted friends, who jump in to be friendly but then drown me out. I'm no good at competing for airtime in conversation, so I can be easily knocked out of the loop.

Nobody would want to be friends with introverts only or extroverts only. A mix is good. But if you suspect you are hanging with extroverts by default, just because they chose you, and the friendships don't feel fulfilling, you might want to find some quiet friends, too. Making friends isn't always easy for introverts, but it's not really something you should outsource. Introverts and extroverts can be friends, of course, if they come to an understanding of each other's nature.

One self-identified extrovert chided me for saying that I had to be "in the mood" for extroverted friends. She said, "I don't have to be 'in the mood' to spend time with my friends, regardless of their intro- or extroversion. Friendship shouldn't be conditional on your mood."

To an extent, this is true. If a friend needed me, I would be there regardless of my mood. But in terms of simple socializing, I respectfully disagree. I suspect this extrovert has no idea what it means to not be in the mood for other people. It's an introvert thing.

Because They Love You

Family members who don't understand your introversion can be tough. They think they know you better than you know yourself, and they often don't edit what they say. After all, you're family! On top of that, criticism from family is hardest to deflect because there will always be little niggling doubts in the back of our minds: Maybe they're right. Maybe they do know me better than I know myself. Maybe I am sullen/shy/sulking/unfriendly/a bitch and I just don't know it. After all, family doesn't just push our buttons—they invented our buttons.

Trying to push back against people who genuinely believe they have your best interests at heart is tough. You don't want to make them feel bad, or start a fight. All you really want to do is sit quietly and read.

I can't tell you how to solve your family issues. There are professionals who make entire careers out of that; I leave the complicated stuff to them. But there are ways you can try to keep the peace and your sanity when your family gets all up in your grill about your introvert ways. The trick is staying solid at your center and not letting them rile you, because the more upset you get, the more righteous they are likely to feel. *See? See how touchy all that time alone makes you?*

If you know you are an introvert, then you know you are an introvert and that's that. You don't have to fight to prove it. Explain yourself if you want, but don't justify yourself. Pick your battles. If you're a teen at home and your mother scolds, "Get out of the house, it's not healthy to spend so much time alone!" you could just get up and leave the house—take a book to a coffee shop or a park or the library. There, you did what she said, but you did it your way. Subversive? You bet. But self-protective, too.

When I was a teenager, I would often lie in bed on weekend mornings and listen until I heard family activity move out of the kitchen so that I could have breakfast in peace. Nowadays, I stay up late, after my early-to-bed husband has departed for dreamland, to get the solitude I need. (I do work alone all day, but that feels different, since I have things tugging at my brain while I work. At night, it's me and the TV and maybe a mindless computer game, as I let my busy brain wind down for sleep.)

The enforced family togetherness that is typical during the holiday season can be especially wearing for introverts. I once had houseguests for a week over the holidays and found myself partly reverting to my old adolescent ways, drinking my first cup of coffee in bed (thanks to my dear husband, who brought it to me) before facing the day's merriment. And I never go on an extended family visit without packing walking shoes. When the walls start closing in on me, I lace them on for "exercise." Nobody can argue with that, it's good for me. I can usually buy an hour of solitude that way.

Sometimes you can hide in plain sight. A crowd can take the pressure off the individual. A family excursion to a mall affords the opportunity to wander off between the clothing racks, retreat into a dressing room, or step alone into a shop. If it's gift-giving season, mysterious allusions to gifts should buy you some alone time. Movies are another escape without escape. You're together, but not. You can either watch the movie or just go to the happy quiet place in your head for a couple of hours.

Then there's the pseudo-sacrifice: supermarket duty, for example. Volunteer to do the grocery shopping or run to the store for that forgotten ingredient, and you can stroll up and down the aisles, numbed by piped-in music, communing with nothing more taxing than Brussels sprouts and canned pumpkin. Chitchat with the checker optional. All that alone time and you can even sell it as a noble gesture.

Sometimes you don't even have to leave the house. Consider the jigsaw puzzle. Set it up and there it sits, offering respite in the middle of whatever chaos might surround it. Sit down to work it and you shift your focus from the people to the puzzle, which never natters or nags. I've also found that knitting helps keep some personal space in my brain during those family-just-sittin'-around times. I can remain cognizant of everything happening around me and participate, but the little task engages the wandering part of my mind and somehow approximates solitude in a crowd. I'm not exactly sure why this bit of voodoo works for me, but it does.

We all want our families to understand and appreciate our

essential nature. And over time, if you quietly and without hostility assert yourself, your loving family is bound to come around and see you as you are. If they don't, that's a pity. But you don't have to make them. You just have to find ways to work around them. No big whoop.

Itty-Bitty Introverts

Cousin Tami was the kind of little girl who would gleefully throw herself in people's arms, with squeals and hugs and joyous enthusiasm. My mother would look at her, and then look at me wistfully. Mom wished I were more like Tami instead of the reserved, even standoffish, little bookworm I was. She even said as much once. "Stiff-necked" is how my father described me.

I thought briefly of trying to be more like Tami (even her name seems more extroverted than mine), but I don't think I ever tried. Really, the idea is so alien and impossible to me, Mom might as well have wanted me to turn into a flying pink unicorn. Curiously, my mother was pretty introverted herself; when she wasn't working, she spent much of her time sitting quietly over her ubiquitous needlework projects.

If we have difficulty accepting introversion in adults, we have five times the trouble accepting it in children. Children are supposed to skip and sing and giggle and throw themselves into people's arms. They're not supposed to take a book into a closet, close the door, and sit on a low stool and read for hours, which was one of my childhood pastimes.

I am appalled by parents who insist their children hug and kiss friends and relatives, and my inclination around children is to sit back and let them warm up to me at their own pace. If that's never, then so be it. Nobody is required to like me and nobody should be forced to pretend. (Besides, isn't forcing children to display affection when they are reluctant teaching them that their bodies aren't their own? Not to get all scary and serious on you, but that's probably not the best lesson for any child.)

I have no children of my own and little contact with kids on a regular basis so I speak mostly as a former child and an observer. In addition, I've heard from many introverts over the years whose parents imbued in them shame for the very essence of who they are.

"My family thinks that there is something wrong with me, psychologically, and they can't seem to fathom why I am at my happiest point when I'm alone," an introvert wrote. "According to my mother, I need to see a therapist immediately before I become depressed."

Another is still affected by comments from her mother about her quietness and lack of friends—even though Mom was introverted, too. "The comments made me even more uncomfortable in social situations as an adult, as I assumed people were judging me if I didn't contribute much."

"I believe I am a God of Awkward Silences," another wrote. "My parents get angry about this, but they don't have a damn clue about what's going on in my head."

I've also heard from parents of introverted children whose teachers express concern for the child's development or mental state.

"My intelligent, introverted son is going overseas on a group trip next week," one introvert wrote. "His group leader has asked me several times if he's ever going to 'loosen up.'"

Another parent was in a state of high anxiety because her child's teacher had recommended an evaluation for Asperger's syndrome.

Obviously, I have no idea if this child has Asperger's and maybe the suggestion is not out of line. But parents needn't panic if their child prefers to play quietly alone rather than with others, or makes just one friend in class rather than developing a posse, or would rather read than climb the monkey bars, or chooses track over a team sport like soccer.

One introverted parent of an introverted son said her son's preschool teacher expressed concern that the child was not interacting with other children much. The teacher feared the boy might be lonely and isolated. "When I asked him about it," the mother wrote, "he said, 'No, Mama, I love being alone!'"

So the question parents should ask themselves if they have a solitary child is, "Does my child seem unhappy?"

Because really, the bottom line: If you're happy alone, why should it surprise you—or anyone else, for that matter—that your child is, too?

To parent an introverted child, you need first of all to be comfortable with your own introversion. Every parent's goal is (or should be) to live by example, so if you feel ashamed of your introversion or try to make yourself a different person, how can you hope to teach your child to be comfortable in his or her quiet place?

It's not hard to unintentionally create self-doubt in a child's mind if you constantly push him out the door to play with others, worry over the quantity of her friendships, or fret if he prefers a family dinner over a big birthday bash with a clown and pin the tail on the donkey. (Does anybody really like clowns? Perhaps they're an extrovert thing, too. And they have the stench of audience participation to them. Protect me from clowns.)

All parents worry about whether their children are happy, and parents tend to be exceedingly sensitive to their children's moods. And since extrovert happiness is much easier to spot and understand than introvert happiness, it's understandable that you might try to push your child to behave in ways that allay your fears. And, of course, if your child is usually social and outgoing and suddenly becomes withdrawn, that's a big red flag, not to be ignored.

But if the little one consistently prefers being solo over social, can spend hours playing alone, loves a good book, a quiet room, and one-on-one time with friends and family, then what you have is a little introvert who should be given plenty of space to do what comes naturally.

Sure, you might want to check in sometimes—poke your head in the door from time to time and ask, "Doing okay?" Open discussion about party invitations. Make sure your child learns the difference between solitude and loneliness and can recognize it. Talk about your own needs and preferences in order to normalize them in your child's perception.

You might also need to run interference with others who

don't understand, like teachers and grandparents. Of course, everyone who worries about your child does so with love and you can only appreciate that. But you might need to explain things your child can't in a way that others will take seriously.

Love your children the way they are and they will love you back in their way—which may or may not involve throwing themselves in your arms with squeals of enthusiasm.

Love Us, but Leave Us Alone (Sometimes)

I n a perfect world, love conquers all, and that's a beautiful sentiment. But alas, we live in an imperfect world and sometimes love needs help. I've heard a lot of sad and stressful stories about introverts and extroverts trying to make love work and failing. Counseling an extrovert who was frustrated with her introverted boyfriend but claimed that otherwise "the fundamentals" of the relationship were good, advice columnist Carolyn Hax said, "I can't think of anything more fundamental than your personalities."

Not to say that the case is hopeless. Introverts and extroverts can live happily ever after. "I am married to an extrovert and I like how she handles all of the stuff that makes me cringe: chitchat, introductions, finding a topic to talk about," said one introvert.

"My wife, an extrovert, and I, an introvert, have been happily married for more than forty years," another man wrote. "One key is working out a mutually satisfactory modus vivendi—I go to some of the events she wants to go to to keep her happy, and we stay home from some of them to keep me happy."

"I sympathize with introverts and can understand that I may be annoying," an extrovert conceded. "The best situation is if I avoid extreme introverts. It does not work. However . . . A degree of introversion is often a pleasant trait."

But many other introverts who wrote into my blog did so with tales of personality-conflict woe.

One wrote that as a college student, she often dated extroverted men. "While the fun of youth was 'fun' as extroverts describe it, as I matured I realized that what I deem to be fun often does not match what many extroverts deem to be fun."

"My ex-husband was an extrovert and could never understand my need for alone time," wrote another. "By wanting all my attention all the time, he never got quite enough.

"After eleven years, this has now cost me a marriage. My husband doesn't (and won't) understand why I am like this. He calls me a hermit. I am, but I don't see it as a bad thing!"

Of course, some of the extroverted spouses just sound like run-of-the-mill losers.

"I am currently separated from my extroverted spouse after years of being put down because he felt I was antisocial, a hermit, lazy, snobby, self-absorbed, you name it—he took every aspect of my introversion and tried to twist it around into making me feel like a terrible person," an introvert wrote.

This, I believe, had nothing to do with her spouse being an extrovert and everything to do with him being a nasty SOB. We are all well-advised to avoid people who put that kind of energy into making us feel bad.

But we want to talk about good people trying to work out differences, and like every long-term relationship, introvert-extrovert relationships require mutual respect, compromise, compassion, and empathy. We need to keep in mind at all times that our way is just one way. Recognizing the differences with no value judgments is the first step to respecting them enough to make a relationship work. And among other things, respect means no eye rolling, no snide remarks, no apologies, no shame. After all, properly managed, introversion and extroversion are a yin and yang that can work for a couple. An extrovert can bring new people into an introvert's life while the introvert can create peaceful spaces in the home and relationship.

You cannot talk an extrovert into needing and wanting less social interaction any more than an extrovert can talk an introvert into wanting more. So we can only let each other be. Extroverts are entitled to the freedom to socialize solo, no guilt trips. Just look at it as a way to get the house to yourself. And if you like deep, intimate conversations with your friends, do you really need your partner there? My husband is more extroverted than I, but the rule in our marriage is that neither of us is required to participate in any social event. Sometimes I go out without my husband; sometimes he goes out without me. By allowing each other freedom most of the time, we can easily be gracious when asked, "pretty please," to do something that doesn't thrill us.

And yes, this might require an explicit discussion, which might sound awkward but can be liberating. One introvert said she and her husband were married several years before they had a talk laying out guidelines for socializing. The stress points for this couple were vacations, which were almost always with friends or visiting friends, and house guests, because they live in an area popular with tourists. "After the talk: Vacations are us only," she wrote. "We can have a few long weekends a year where we visit and/or travel with friends, but the *real* vacations must be friend-free. We can have weekend guests once a month. (This is too much for me, but it's a compromise.)"

So laying out some parameters is job one. From there, we are responsible for our own comfort out of our comfort zone. So you don't want to go to your sweetie's office holiday party? If sweetie *really* wants you there, then gut up and make the best of it. Maybe parties will be easier if you decide ahead of time how long you will stay. Or take two cars, so that you can bail whenever you want. Maybe getting to know new people will be easier if you plan to do something—a museum or street fair—rather than sitting around making self-conscious getting-to-know-you conversation. Weekends with the in-laws can be easier to manage if you know your partner will cover for you when you need to duck out for quiet time. Again, this will entail some frank discussion, but one good discussion can preclude a million tense situations.

The phone, too, can be a surprising source of tension. Must one person answer every ring because the other doesn't want to? My husband uses his cell phone exclusively, so if I don't feel like answering our home phone (as is the case 97.9 percent of the time), he doesn't care. And while he will email during the day for necessary discussions (such as dinner), I call sometimes, too, since that's more convenient for him—although he agrees that I'm terrible on the telephone.

As much as you love being with the person you love, if you have high need for quiet time, that also needs to be negotiated.

My husband is an early bird and I'm a night owl, so we each get daily solitude that way. I also travel alone on business and he doesn't mind being a bachelor occasionally. Actually, he kinda likes it. You don't have to apologize for this, but you do need to be gracious about it. For example, insist on quiet time after work if you need it, but your partner should then get your undivided attention for equal time. If you have kids, which we do not, you have another layer to the negotiation. Perhaps the extroverted spouse can take over child duties each day for a period of time when the introvert most needs a few moments of silence.

Your extrovert may need an explicit explanation of what alone means to you, one introvert learned. "It turned out that her definition of 'alone time' was 'alone with family' (as in, me and, later, our daughter) and she was seriously hurt by my need to be alone from them as well," he wrote.

Introverts and extroverts might even need to figure out how to argue productively. When we started dating, my husband made me promise that I would never write what I need to say in a letter, which had long been my preferred mode of communicating difficult information to friends and loved ones. I'll admit, this rule has been a little hobbling for me. I am much more comfortable writing than speaking. A couple of times I've actually written a letter and read it to him. But if letters are that threatening to him, and they are, then it is to my benefit to avoid them, especially in situations that are already sensitive.

Another introvert explained how she and her extroverted husband came to terms with differing communication styles. "He doesn't understand that I need to process how I feel first and then put that into words. From his perspective, he thinks that I am shutting down and not willing to work on the issue. Over time, we've been able to adjust to each other's styles. He gives me alone time to work the issue out first, and I try to verbalize what I'm thinking as much as possible."

The good news is mixed marriages are not impossible. All they require are tolerance, an open mind, and ground rules.

I F#&$ing Hate It When They Say That

The title of this chapter is a quote from actress Kristen Stewart, who became famous as Bella Swan in the *Twilight* movies. Stewart got all kinds of grief after an appearance on *Oprah* because she seemed awkward. She's also been criticized because she hates being stalked by paparazzi and generally doesn't seem to enjoy the pander-to-the-public aspect of her acting career. Not only that, but some of her fans and followers seem to feel that she owes them something—that because she has become famous in her chosen field, they are justified in demanding her soul. People insist that because Stewart won't gush intimate details of her life on *Oprah*, because she finds the red-carpet experience overwhelming and unpleasant, because she tries to maintain some semblance of privacy, she is failing in her role as movie star.

And that pisses Stewart off.

"I hate it when they say I'm ungrateful, and I f#&$ing hate it when they say I don't give a sh*t, because nobody cares more than I do," she said.

Yes indeed. We appear mild-mannered and we're not usually ones to gripe in public, but introverts can be as surly as the next guy. We get annoyed by assumptions made about us and behaviors directed at us. We're not always as outspoken as Stewart (though we applaud her candor) because we don't feel like getting into it, but our thoughts are throwing daggers.

Like being called stuck-up or snobby. That annoys me and it hurts my feelings. Just because introverts don't chatter at anyone near earshot does not mean we have judged people and found them wanting. Sometimes we are in listening mode. Or we don't have anything to say. Or our minds are someplace else. There's nothing inherently sinister about our silence.

We hate being told we hate people. That's not true and it makes us sound mean. We like people, especially people we like. We prefer people in small numbers and controlled doses because we like people so much, we want to actually get to know them.

We hate being accused of not knowing how to have fun. The implied insult there (or is it overt?) is that we're drips. Wet blankets. Just because fun for introverts isn't raucous, some people get confused. Phooey.

"Why are you so quiet?" rubs on our nerves. What is the correct answer to that question and why does it sound so accusatory? "That's just the way I am" would seem to be self-evident, but apparently not. It's my go-to response, although in my head I might be saying, as one introvert suggested, "Someone has to be."

I was once accused of having nothing to say, which is a bare-knuckle lie. The accusation was leveled at me by a friend with much too much to say. In a way, he was correct, since I usually was so overwhelmed by his tsunami of words, I was struck dumb. I couldn't even remember what I might have wanted to say if I'd had a chance. But to him, because words did not explode from my head, I must not have anything to say.

Despite our quiet demeanor, we're not necessarily angry or bored. We're just sitting here minding our own business. Why can't people let a face be? But they can't. "Why are you so serious?" is the corollary to one of our least favorites, *"Smile!"* or, even more grating, a happy trill to *"Turn that frown upside down!"*

"People tend to assume that if you're not grinning like an idiot all the time, you're unhappy," griped one introvert. Another suggested responding that though we're serious on the outside, in our heads, there's a party going on.

Speaking of parties, we resent the implication that we poop them. And even if we did, the only party we poop is our own. Everyone else is free to do whatever they please, party-wise. Also, *"Oh, come on!"* is not the correct response when we are pooping a party. Grabbing our arm and trying to drag us into it does not improve the situation. We f#&$ing hate that.

In general, we f#&$ing hate when people try to bully or shame us into behaving in ways that are counter to our nature. And they may not know it, but people who push their luck are risking us going all Kristen Stewart on their asses.

A Team of One

Know what introverts hate? Team-building exercises. Know what else? Brainstorming sessions. Also standing up in meetings and telling everyone a little bit about themselves. And being told that they're not a team player because they'd rather go home after work than to happy hour with the gang from accounting.

Much of what we "know" about getting ahead in business, about managing people, about building successful teams is clearly developed by extroverts, for extroverts. "Everybody knows" charismatic leaders are better leaders. Brainstorming sessions are the optimum way to solve problems and generate fresh ideas. The best employees are team players.

I'll stick my neck out and say there's not an introvert alive who can think clearly in free-for-all brainstorming sessions. My tendency in this sort of situation is to retreat into my own head rather than roll around in other peoples' ideas. (Does anyone listen to anyone else in sessions like that? Seems like they're all too busy shouting out their ideas. It's like Twitter—everyone bellowing into a crowd.) Even if I do get an idea worth sharing, I have a hard time getting it out there. My mouth opens and shuts, opens and shuts, interjecting random syllables that get lost in the hubbub, until the idea flees from my brain. I take a lot of notes in meetings—things to think about later, or ideas that come to mind that might be worth pursuing afterward, outside the team chaos.

It's not that introverts aren't good team players. We just don't need to be in the same room as the rest of the team at all times. We would much prefer to have part of the project carved out for us to squirrel away with it in our offices, consulting as necessary but working independently.

The workplace might be the most important place for introverts to assert themselves and find ways to tap into their strengths. Otherwise, we are competing professionally on an uneven playing field, trying to play the extrovert game against people who are natural-born extroverts. Extroverts may be better at making a first impression, so introverts have to look for other ways to get under the boss's skin. In a good way.

For one thing, introverts need to figure out what they do best, and make sure the boss knows. After a brainstorming session where you were steamrollered, maybe hit up your boss for a one-on-one meeting to contribute your ideas. Or write a pithy memo. Volunteer to do the things you know you do well, like writing up reports. Volunteering shows your team spirit, and it means you won't be assigned extrovert-style tasks.

And if you conduct much of your business via email, is that so bad? We are told it is. But I'm terrible on the phone; I make a much better impression in writing or in person. Why would I want to rely on my weakness rather than my strengths?

Sometimes you have to find least-painful ways to do most-painful things. Like conferences, which can be introvert torture. All those people for days and days, the expectation that you will work the room and make new contacts. Marketing pro and introvert Lisa Petrilli recommends that introverts set up meetings with people they want to meet before a conference starts. That gives you good reason not to bail out on attending sessions, and you can network one-on-one, without having to plunge into a crowd with handshakes and your best extrovert smile. (Or is that a grimace?) And maybe if you take breakfast meetings, you can allow yourself to bow out of evening cocktails. Plus, it might give you someone to walk into the day's first session with, making the entrance a little easier if you're the nervous type.

Back at the office, fitting introvert ways into the company culture sometimes means just speaking up. "In general, I prefer email to the phone, will that work for you?" Or "I don't do my best thinking in meetings, but I'd like to get back to you with some ideas." Just get it out there, no big whoop. A good manager will appreciate the candor and intentions, especially when you do a good job. A good manager also will appreciate that your reluctance to schmooze everyone in the office makes you productive. And a good manager will understand (if you explain) that a closed office door isn't meant to be unfriendly. Eventually you might even be able to persuade that manager that team-building games are not necessary in every single sales meeting.

And if you don't have an office door to close? Unfortunately, many modern offices are an anathema to introverts—the dreaded open office, the privacy-sucking cubicle. Thinking can be so difficult for us when we are forced to hear everyone else's phone conversations, when we are helpless to prevent the office gossip from stopping by our desk for a little jaw wag, when silence and solitude are all but impossible to come by.

If you're an unhappy introverted cubicle dweller, you'll have to come up with solutions that fit your office culture. Can you wear noise-canceling headphones? Or, less conspicuously, earbuds hooked up to an MP3 player—either playing music or playing nothing? Can you shift your hours to have time in an empty office before everyone arrives or after everyone is gone? Maybe you can move into an empty conference room when you have work that requires concentration. Maybe you can work at home sometimes. When I worked at a newspaper—a place that by nature buzzes and bustles (at least it did back in the days when newspapers were flourishing)—I did most of my writing at home, with the blessing of my boss.

Taking breaks can help; walk around the building or the block to let your brain air out. Take yourself to lunch alone, or brown-bag it and dine solo in a peaceful spot. (Is there a park nearby? Perfect.) You can even resort to catching a few minutes' peace sitting in your car. And of course, if all else fails, there's the bathroom, which works as well on the job as it does at parties.

And don't worry—being an introvert doesn't necessarily mean that you're doomed to the cubicle forever. There could be a corner office in your future, because introversion as an impediment to leadership is another workplace myth being debunked. Researchers are finding that introverted leadership is not inferior, it's just different. One study says that different types of teams perform best under different types of leaders. Research at 130 franchise restaurants found that extroverts are good at leading teams that just want to be told what to do, introverts are good at leading teams in which everyone contributes ideas. Introverts listen, extroverts expound. Extroverts need external approval to stay motivated; introverts are internally motivated.

One of introverts' liabilities or strengths, depending on the situation or who you ask, is that we are slow to make decisions. We have to consider and deliberate before we act. If a team needs quick action, it needs an extrovert. But an introverted leader can help focus and manage the energy of an extroverted team.

Research is fuzzy on whether charismatic leaders are actually more effective for the bottom line. Charismatic leaders might get a lot of attention because that's what charismatic people do best. Extroverts get their ideas out to the world, but also can be loose cannons. You never know what they'll say. Introverts think carefully before they speak. We can be excellent public speakers because we prepare carefully.

Extroverts might be more willing to leap into bold change than introverts, who want to think things through thoroughly. These great leaps can be exciting and give the impression of progress, but which approach actually, consistently gets better results? We don't know for sure, but I bet in the end, it's a wash.

So ignore common wisdom about the superior leadership qualities of extroverts, and instead, figure out your strengths and use 'em, sell 'em, and don't apologize for 'em.

Introvert Feats of Derring-Do

Y ou're not an introvert."

I've heard those words a million times from people familiar with my dog and pony show. I understand their confusion. When I set those plates spinning, I'm performing what I think of as an introvert feat of derring-do.

My dog and pony show is just one astounding introvert feat. Some of my other stunts of social derring-do are online. I maintain a lively social life via email and social networking. And, in a way, writing books, articles, and blogs is a type of performance, one that suits many introverts well.

Introverts are not incapable of performing and having large personalities—online, on-screen, or onstage. Steve Martin, a public clown, is famously introverted, as were Johnny Carson and Katharine Hepburn. Julia Roberts identifies herself as an introvert. In a memoir, Françoise Gilot, one of Pablo Picasso's many paramours, described the artist as a "bombastic introvert."

Introverts can act, sing, and dance, onstage and in public. But performing in character is entirely different from performing at a party. Some introverted actors find the character within them; others put on a character or persona like body armor. Actually, that's what many introverts do when we have to step out of our quiet comfort zone.

Public speaking—widely acknowledged as the most common phobia—also is no sweat for me and many other introverts. This is, in part, because of the controlled circumstances. Public speaking is not an interaction; it is a one-way conversation where we are guaranteed to get our say. And introverts tend to prepare well. We show up already knowing what we want to say and don't have to wing it or take chances. We know what we have to say, we say it, badabing, badaboom. Done. Actually, the pre- and post-speech meet and greets are more stressful for me than the speech itself.

People insist swashbuckling introverts cannot possibly be introverts because we can be charming or, at the very least, communicative. They have us confused with shrinking violets, with shy people. For some people, the difference seems to be very difficult to grasp—the word "shy" springs to their lips again and again, no matter how many times I correct them.

It's hard to know what to make of this. I suppose the connection between introverted and shy has been solidly planted in people's minds so long, it's hard to uproot. Perhaps a little imagery would help. Introverts are actually a lot like Clark Kent—mild and unassuming much of the time, but able to swoop in and turn on our Supercharm when we choose.

First, Leave the House and Other Tips for Making Friends

Some people have never met a stranger. They make friends wherever they go and collect people like others collect books. These people are a mighty force, awesome to watch in action. They can enter a room and within minutes make contact of some sort with everyone in it. By the end of a party, they have nicknames for half the guests and inside jokes with the other half. Their phones ring continually, and when they're looking for people to do stuff with, they have a long list to choose from.

Boy, is that not me.

Sure, I can talk to people pretty easily when I choose, and I'm approachable, also when I choose. But that's schmoozing. From party to chat to friend is an enormous distance, difficult to traverse, requiring time and effort that may or may not pay off—especially for those of us who seek depth in our friendships, and even more especially for postadolescents. My youthful days of meeting someone and being BFFs within hours are long gone.

These days I'm slow and cautious and discern between friends and acquaintances.

Introverts might not need people as much as extroverts, which is to say that we don't need random people who just fill up space. But we do need friends. We need people to call when we want company, in whom we can confide when we need a sympathetic ear (and to whom we can provide the same service), and with whom we can feel one hundred percent ourselves. But making friends can be oh so hard for introverts.

First of all, we set the bar pretty high for friendship. What an extrovert might call a friend, we'd call an acquaintance. Also, it's hard to make friends when you're not inclined to spend time out and about. We don't encounter many new people in our living rooms. So step one for making friends: Leave the house.

Sometimes this feels like a sacrifice. Staying home is so much easier. Second easiest is going out with people we know well—old friends and family. But sometimes we find ourselves in a friend deficit for one reason or another and the only way to remedy that is to accept invitations and get out among new people as often as we can. I know, I know. The very idea makes me want to take a nap. But nothing good comes without sacrifice.

If you're shy among groups, there's nothing wrong with latching onto someone who isn't and riding along. Science says so. Researchers call that person a "surrogate" and one study in Japan found that after seven months, shy students entering a university who used a surrogate had as many friends as not-shy students.

I've also had good luck mining my past. Some of my most gratifying new friendships are old friendships—people I knew long ago but with whom I lost touch. (Thank you, Internet.) Actually, although some were long-ago friends, others were acquaintances in the past who became friends in the present. Still others—often people from my high school days—I knew on sight but never exchanged two words with until we were thrown together in the present. Shared past is very powerful and reminiscing helped fast-forward us through some of the most awkward getting-to-know-you stuff.

Because, let's face it, making friends can be awkward. I mean, what do you do when you meet someone you'd like to be friends with? "Wanna be my friend?" doesn't work for anyone past the age of seven. But you still have to be a little bit pushy, make contact, extend invitations. And that feels awkward. I tell myself that what feels pushy to me might just seem friendly to others. As introverts, our sensitivity can work for us or against us. We don't want be so sensitive that we're afraid to take chances. On the other hand, we do have to be sensitive enough to recognize if and when it's time to give up.

Mostly, though, you have to just soldier through the awkwardness of the early stages of friendship. How often can you extend invitations without seeming needy? How long can you let go between invitations without seeming uninterested? How would a last-minute invitation go over? At what point are you tight enough to text? There are no definitive answers to any of these questions—although caution is always advisable. An invitation every couple of weeks to start, perhaps. Texting with a purpose only ("running late" or "meet me at the entrance") until a true connection is established. I've even had an explicit discussion about last-minute invitations with one potential new friend, and we agreed that they are welcome.

Insta-friendship rarely happens once we're past adolescence. Friendship is cumulative and so (exhausting though it may sound) when we meet someone with friend potential, we have to put in the time. Fake it till we make it. If the friendship is meant to be, that gratifying "click" of real connection will happen eventually.

I find that if I lower my expectations of friendships and ratchet back my intensity in the beginning, the friendships are more likely to grow (or not) naturally. You can't force it. Some friendships look promising but fizzle quickly, some that I didn't expect or think much about at first deepen slowly. It's just a matter of going into them quietly to see what happens. When I'm shopping for friends I keep a lot of superficial connections going, put in the time, and wait to see which take root. New friendships can never take the place of solid old ones, but they can provide exciting new vistas.

On the other hand, sometimes, you just have to know when to fold 'em. This also is not a reflection on anyone. We all want the same thing: connection. Nobody is a failure when friendships fail to kick in, so we have to just cut our losses, skip the self-flagellation, and move on to the next interesting person. There are plenty of potential friends out there, if you leave the house.

Mind Fullness to Mindfulness

You'd think that with all the time we spend in our own minds, introverts would be mindfulness gurus. But when you think about it further—maybe not. Mindfulness actually is the opposite of introverts' full minds. Mindfulness is opening up your mind to what is really happening around you. It's feeling the air, hearing the birds, tasting your food, appreciating the moment, being present to the present.

Introverts are not always so good at that. When your mind is spinning with interesting thoughts, you're not actually in touch with what is going on around you. You're looking out at the world through holes in your head rather than being fully in it. And do you ever find yourself with something churning in your head that is so insistent that allowing yourself to just fall into the whirlpool of thoughts is easier than silencing them? Do you find that keeping thoughts at bay requires huge exertion?

That's kind of what's happening. Neurologists talk about

something called the default-mode network (DMN). As I understand it, this is the neural activity our minds slip into when we're not making them do something else. And that default activity is usually what they call daydreaming, what I'd call thinking. (What's the difference between daydreaming and thinking?) Introverts' DMN is way deep inside our own minds, where there's often a lot going on. We may be quiet people in a noisy world, but we're internally noisy. And that's not mindfulness. That's full-mindedness, perhaps.

I've been practicing yoga for several years. At the end of every class is a five-minute relaxation, savasana. You lie on your back, in what some people call corpse pose, and let yourself completely relax. Easy, right? Yeah, except relaxing my mind. More often than not, my brain starts whirring furiously the moment we lie down, and the savasana ends before I'm even aware it's going on. In one class, my teacher leads us through a relaxation, but sometimes I can barely hear her over my own thoughts. That's not mindfulness.

Same thing when I walk my dog. The trees are green, the birds are singing, and I'm looking at the ground, furiously thinking about whatever it is I'm thinking about. The more my brain whirs, the faster I walk, until I'm dragging the dog behind me like a pull toy. I usually catch myself at some point during the walk. I'll take a breath, look around, feel the sun, try to be present in the moment. That lasts for a few minutes. Then, before I even realize it, I'm back in my busy brain.

But letting your own thoughts interfere with being in the present is no better than letting outside noise intrude on your peace. Unfortunately, it's a lot easier to turn off the TV or close the door on noise than it is to turn down the volume in your head. It's no mystery why meditation is considered a discipline.

Our busy minds are a form of energy we have to learn to manage. We need to harness our brains' power for our own good, and calm it when it gets too frenetic. And yeah, we can feel frenetic even sitting alone and silent in a quiet room.

I had an interesting experience at a party once. It was my own party, a brunch, which I anticipated with the usual combination of pleasure, high anxiety, and preemptive exhaustion. But this time, while I prepared the food, I also prepared myself by thinking about how I could manage my psychic energy.

Because I went into the party conscious of my energy, an interesting thing happened: I was talking to a guest, someone I didn't know well, and suddenly realized that my mind was shooting every which way. Part of it was focused on the conversation, yes. But I also was conscious of other conversations around me. I was aware of my husband manning the barbecue. I was wondering about guests who hadn't arrived yet. Keeping an eye on the dog. Thinking about running back into the house for . . . what? I didn't even know.

No wonder social events exhaust me! My poor brain, accustomed to the quiet focus of solitude, wasn't processing my environment efficiently. It was trying to absorb and interpret too much, giving me that familiar my-head-might-explode feeling. But this time, as soon as I became aware of my scattered energy, I tried to gather it in and focus entirely on the conversation at hand. I tried to be mindful of what I was doing at that moment, which was having a conversation. Immediately, calm settled over me. I looked at the woman talking to me, who a moment earlier was irritating as a buzzing fly, and became interested in what she was saying. The rest of the party receded to the background and managed to function without me for the ten minutes I permitted myself to focus. I was infinitely more relaxed than I had been a minute earlier.

Having a busy mind is both a benefit and a liability. Our busy minds keep us from getting bored, they help us be creative, they are in many ways the essence of who we are. But sometimes the racket inside our heads is loud as a car alarm, interfering with our ability to connect with the world around us, to focus on the task at hand, or to get a good night's sleep. And our busy minds also can stress us out and make us unhappy. In one study, researchers used an iPhone app to check in on people at random points throughout the day and found that the more people were thinking about something other than what they were doing, the less happy they felt. Even when they weren't thinking about anything particularly bad.

I don't suggest cultivating mindfulness is easy and I have no new ideas to reach it. Who am I to try to improve on what Buddhists have done for thousands of years? I only suggest that this is something introverts might want to think about. And then, stop thinking.

Mistakes Introverts Make

We are all so very wonderful and yet—I'm sorry, but it must be said—we are not perfect. This book has focused mostly on staking out turf in our culture for introverts, but now it's time to consider some things related to our introversion that might be interfering with our relationships and accomplishments. Many or most of us have probably made some of these mistakes at one time or another. I certainly have.

Isolating: Yes, some people need more social interaction than others. But to be healthy and fully rounded human beings, we all need some and we need it on a regular basis. Too much isolation is not healthy. I know it's time to leave the house when I start feeling gloomy in my solitude, or like I'm getting weird. Weird is subjective, but when going to the supermarket feels like a major excursion, when I start worrying that I may have lost the ability to converse, when I get furious at near-strangers in my online social networks, I know it's time for face time. I call a friend, do

lunch, attend a party . . . anything to get my social gears cranking again. It needn't be anything deep and meaningful. Just a
little something to reconnect me.

Not returning phone calls: It's perfectly okay to ask others to
respect and honor our loathing for the telephone, but healthy relationships are a two-way street. We don't get carte blanche to ignore all phone calls. When someone you care about calls—even if
you let it go to voice mail to deal with later—you really should
respond at some point. If necessary, drop an email and schedule
the call. Otherwise, pick up the phone and dial. (An exception: If
someone obstinately refuses any other form of communication
and insists on frequent time-sucking phone calls, then you get
some leeway to make your point.)

Plunging into the deep end: As much as we prefer deep conversation, plunging straight into your worldview over the onion
dip at a party can be off-putting to others. As awkward as you
might feel about it, chitchat is the way to wade into the shallows.
If the conversation "takes," then you can ease into the deep. If
you're looking for friends, remember that rushing the conversation
isn't a shortcut. Friendships build incrementally, and they start
with small talk.

Letting your mouth run away with you: Ah, the dreaded babble. It happens. Lots of us chatter when we're nervous. Shy introverts might be prone to this. It's like running down a hill; once
you get started, it's hard to slow down. But it also might happen
when the subject is something you are particularly passionate
about. Either you get caught up in your own enthusiasm, or you
burrow deep into your own knowledge and forget to check audience reaction. If you suddenly realize you've careened into a long

monologue, take a breath and look around. Do people appear rapt? Then continue. Do they look glazed or slightly pained? My favorite line at that point is, "But don't get me started . . ." Cue laughter, everything's fine.

Confusing introversion and fear: We all must do things we don't like. That's life. But if you find that you *can't* bring yourself to do certain things, like return a phone call, attend a gathering, or join a conversation, then what you're feeling may be fear, not introversion. Fear is a useful emotion, of course, with deep evolutionary roots. But if it interferes with your life and you find yourself regretting things not done, maybe it's time to rummage around in your psyche (one of our favorite activities!) to figure out what you're scared of and how to change that.

Leaning on too few people: We are proud of our insistence on quality over quantity of friendships, but this comes with the risk of putting all our friendship eggs in one or two friends' baskets. Or our significant other's. Or our family's. If you call on the same one or two people again and again when you crave company, you risk appearing needy or, in fact, being needy. Are you at a loss for company when your BFF is busy? Do you feel possessive and maybe even jealous of that one person you feel understands you? Does every get-together have to be deep and meaningful, to the point where just plain fun seems like a waste of time? You might be putting a lot of pressure on your few friends without even realizing it.

This mistake also may leave you lonely if something happens to a friendship—someone moves to another city, finds a new BFF, or you have a falling out. Suddenly you're faced with that stressful chore of making new friends from scratch. With a larger circle of people to draw on, you have more options for deepening an existing superficial friendship.

Judging: Some introverts insist that parties are pointless, chatting is a waste of time, and extroverts are shallow. I neither share nor endorse those opinions. Parties can be joyous, and community ritual has been important throughout history. Small talk connects us and greases the gears of society. And while I'm sure some extroverts are shallow, I'm sure some introverts are as well. Thinking a lot doesn't automatically make you deep. It depends on what you're thinking about. A blanket dismissal of extroverts is bigoted and, well, shallow.

Just 'cause I don't like something doesn't mean it's bad.

Affirmations for Introverts

t's one thing to recognize your needs and vow to assert them, but actually standing up for yourself is another matter altogether. It's just not easy. In the short term, going along to get along is a lot less stressful. Establishing introvert territory doesn't have to be a contentious process, but it may at times require firmness, both with others and with yourself.

To effect change you need a goal, and our goal is to live the introvert's way. But what is that? What does it look like? This is something we each have to decide for ourselves. What is your image of a life well lived as an introvert? Where should you assert yourself, where should you push yourself? Where do you lack boundaries, and with whom? Is it the telephone? Parties? Do you feel misunderstood by friends and family? Have you let others convince you that introversion is a liability? Are you allowing other people to manage your social life?

These questions can help identify our goals. From there, we

have to figure out how to reach them (understanding, of course, that these kinds of goals can be fluid). Research has shown that when it comes to reaching goals, we're better off keeping our eye on the "why" rather than the "how." How you reach a goal is complicated and may change over time. Plans come and go—some succeed, some fail. But the real key to persevering is not some sort of definitive plan, but motivation. Why do you want to change the status quo? Keep your image of the introvert's life in view and it will help set your path to change.

But the change itself—that happens one step at a time. It's little decisions every day, and each decision requires a little conviction, a little starch in the spine, a refusal to be swayed either by other people or by scolding voices in your own head. And sometimes, we need mantras, affirmations we can use to drown those voices out. Here are a few to get you started.

Staying home is doing something. Time spent alone is not negative space. It has its own purposes, both in what you do with it and in what it does for you.

My presence is a gift, not a requirement. If you receive an invitation to do something that doesn't sound fun, you might choose to do it anyway. And that would be very nice of you. But you don't have to.

I like who I like. You are not required to like everyone, and just because you don't like everyone doesn't mean you hate people. It's not your problem if a person is a bore or a boor.

Listening to bores is not my job. Just because you're a good listener doesn't mean you are obligated to listen to anyone who wants to bend your ear. Your listening skills are a gift to be bestowed on only the deserving. You owe it to yourself and loved ones to preserve your limited energy for them and not waste it on people you don't like.

Managing my energy is a favor to myself and everyone around me. Don't let anyone tell you that you're being mean when you step away from the fun. They obviously don't know how cranky you get if you push yourself too hard.

Saying no can be a kindness. If you say no to them, then they may say no to you. Sooner or later they will realize what a blessing the freedom to say no is. Plus, if you say yes when you want to say no, you probably won't present your best self and you might not be much fun.

I can love other people and still not be responsible for their good time. Sometimes you will do things you don't want to do just as a kindness to someone you love. But you don't have to do that all the time.

Just because I'm quiet doesn't mean I have nothing to say. Some people are raconteurs who can hold a room full of people in their thrall. If you're not, oh well. You have plenty to say when the time and circumstances are right for you.

Putting on my dog and pony show is optional. I've been known to panic if conversation is stilted among a group of people, and that puts me into dog and pony overdrive. But I've started giving myself permission to just let things be if I don't feel like putting on a show. This makes socializing much easier. When I felt compelled to put on my extrovert face every time I went out, socializing seemed like too much trouble.

A ringing phone is not a mandate. Some people can't ignore a ringing telephone. You can. And that's fine. Just because somebody wants to talk to you *right now* doesn't mean you are obligated to indulge them.

I know what I need better than anyone else. Yes, they love you. Yes, their intentions are good. Yes, sometimes their suggestions are useful. But even your most intimate intimates don't know you better than you know yourself and you are allowed to weigh their suggestions against your self-knowledge and dismiss them if they don't feel right. No fuss and confrontation necessary, just stay centered and calm and own your own choices.

Other people's desire for me to participate is not more important than my desire not to participate. No matter how much someone wants you to do something, no matter how much pressure that person puts on you, that other person's needs and desires are not automatically more important than your own. You may choose to accede to the other person's wishes, but you also may choose to go your own way. This does not make you a mean person. It makes you your own person.

Middle Ground

A good friend who lives in another city told me that she respects my dislike for the phone and doesn't call unless absolutely necessary. And that made me feel surprisingly bad.

She and I email all day, forwarding articles of interest, exchanging one-liners, discussing the important matters of the day. So that's great. It's like having a good friend in the next cubicle, even though the cubicle is two hundred miles away and neither of us is actually in a cubicle. But I know she also likes a good phone chat and I feel bad that she has completely deferred to my preference. When I realized what was happening, I called her. Just picked up the phone and called. Just like that. And it was good.

Some of my other faraway friends acknowledge and respect my dislike of the phone, but basically say, "Tough noogies, we gotta talk sometimes." If they call and I absolutely don't have time, I don't pick up. Mostly I do, though. Well, now I do, after offending another very dear friend whom I kept intending to call back but just didn't, until he'd left two or three messages. That was just crappy of me. No excuse. I apologized profusely and started picking up any time I saw his number on caller ID. And he, in turn, doesn't gripe if I can't stay on the phone long.

Other friends are fine with scheduling calls, as I prefer, so we do that. In that case, I block out at least an hour for the call— enough time for us to complete preliminary prattle and get to talking. And that is good.

Because many of us fall somewhere in the middle of the introvert/extrovert continuum, we need to find ways for our lives to reflect that. We don't want to opt out of more extroverted activities altogether, nor do we think it's fair to expect our desires to take priority over everyone else's. But there's a learn-and-adjust phase to finding comfortable middle ground. The trick is to start teasing apart the elements of specific activities that you like, and what you particularly don't like.

Interestingly, I've found that taking control over my relationship with the telephone has made it less abhorrent to me. I answer it more often, and initiate calls more often. (Still rarely, but more often.) I've even given out my cell phone number to a couple of people. I also discovered Skype. A friend and I made an appointment and yeah, we both put on a little makeup, tried to look nice. (We both work at home and that can get pretty ugly.) It was fun. I saw her living room, which I'd never seen; she saw my office. By the end of the call, we were running back and forth to our bedrooms to show each other new shoes we'd bought. It was a blast.

So, another piece of information for me: I'm more uncomfortable than I thought with the disembodied voice on a telephone. Now I've found an alternative.

My most outgoing friend—one of those never-met-a-stranger types—can exhaust me when we're out together, but we've found middle ground, too. I love that she brings a party everywhere she goes, and that she understands that I might want to sit in the corner anyway. One night I met up with her and a large gang of her friends at a club. While she gadded about in her way, I spent the evening talking to one woman with whom I'd connected. It was perfect middle ground. I had my kind of fun, my friend had her kind of fun, and she was tickled to death to see me make a new friend.

As I move to middle ground, my friends are, too. The friend who hates typing is trying to email more rather than always using the telephone. Because I don't accept every party invitation, when I do choose to go to a party, it's with pleasure, and nobody hassles me when I'm ready to leave. My husband and friends recognize when a too-large group of people is putting me into an introvert stupor and when I drift away, physically or mentally, they let me. They know I can take care of myself and that I'll be back when I'm ready.

Middle ground is very comfortable. It's a group of six rather than twelve. A welcome telephone chat rather than a reluctant one. It's just enough party and not a minute more. It's a place where I am as comfortable as other people, and vice versa. It's a little trial and error, a little adjusting here and there, a little giving and a little taking. But when we get to middle ground, it is good.

C'mon People Now, Smile on Your Brother

A lot of introverts feel put out because we've been told our way is wrong for so long, we almost believed it ourselves. Now we're figuring out that our way is as valid as the extrovert's, and we feel resentful about the line we've been fed all these years about how we *should* behave if we were healthy, loving, engaged people. That's annoying. Sometimes infuriating. And we're kind of pissed off.

I've heard a lot of venting and name-calling from introverts.

"I have a very low tolerance for being around people for so long, especially idiots . . ."

"Maybe we should start turning the tables on those annoying extroverts and make them explain why they are so superficial and needy."

"I am puzzled and pity those that can't be alone, or depend on others so much for their self-worth or self-actualization."

"[A]re extroverts simply incapable of being quiet?"

I say: It's time to stop the hate.

Of course, all introverts don't hate extroverts, and all extroverts don't believe they possess the secret of the universe. But I've heard enough stories of misunderstanding and animosity to believe it's time to call for hands across the personality divide. We reject the myth that extroversion is better than introversion, and so we must also reject any idea that introversion is better than extroversion.

Part of the problem might be that we (admit it) may have suffered some extrovert envy over the years. I'm certainly guilty of that. I'm envious of the way extroverts can electrify a room and light up everyone around them. I'm envious of their effortless manner in putting people at ease. I'm envious of their lack of inhibitions (when I'm not mildly embarrassed by them). And I'm envious of the way extroversion is rewarded. The world opens its arms to extroverts but steps cautiously around introverts.

Is that the way we want it? Have we done this to ourselves? Does introversion equal prickly? Sure, we want space, but not the wide berth some people give us. Is there a middle ground where we may have our quiet space without assumptions made as to our nature?

Seeing the rewards extroverts want is easy: They want contact, they want to be heard, they want as many connections as they can have. That's easy for people to respond to. The rewards introverts seek are less obvious, and so we sometimes feel like we're missing out. And that, too, makes us a little angry. But we can't *blame* extroverts for this. After all, isn't that exactly what we claim to abhor in extroverts—that they look to other people for validation?

The theme of this book, what I hope you've taken away, is that introversion is simply another way of being from extroversion and that it is up to us to recognize it, accept it, and learn to live the way we feel most comfortable and complete. We want to respect our own introversion, and we ask others to respect it. But— the important but—that means we have to give equal respect to extroversion.

The beauty of this is that when the yin and yang of introversion and extroversion are in harmony, we create a balance in the world: thought and action, silence and sound, stillness and motion. Too much of one or the other, and things go out of whack. Perhaps the dominance of extroversion has allowed American society to become a shouting match, but would a fully introverted culture, with everyone sitting quietly behind closed doors, be able to accomplish anything? Even in China, a generally more introverted culture than America, people are finding their voice, if for no other reason than to speak out to a government that doesn't always speak for them.

When we identify and live true to our nature, we find comfort and grace, and life is suddenly simple. (As simple as life can be, anyway.) When we are confident in our introversion, we can enjoy the chatter and razzle-dazzle of extroverts without feeling angry or threatened by it. And when we assert ourselves without defensiveness, extroverts will learn to accept and appreciate the calm we carry with us.

And all will be right with the world.

Acknowledgments

I am forever indebted to Jenna Schnuer, who smacked me upside the head and said, "Write about introversion!" when *Psychology Today* invited me to blog for them, thereby launching my career as a professional introvert. Thanks, too, to Michael Yessis and Jim Benning, who ran my first essay on introversion on their excellent website *World Hum* and immediately started urging me to write a book on the subject.

Many thanks to my agent, Penny Nelson, who helped me craft and recraft my proposal, with great ideas and cheerful enthusiasm. Equally effusive thanks to my editor, Meg Leder, who saw through the book proposal I thought editors would want to see to the book that I really wanted to write. Working with her has been nothing but delightful.

Meryl Gross has been an invaluable cheerleader and reader, with many exceedingly wise suggestions. Lesley Gaspar, fellow introvert, also has been immeasurably helpful as a reader, both of the blog and the manuscript. And for plain old support, and patience (especially through my whiny years, when writing wasn't treating me particularly well), boatloads of love and gratitude to my friends David Baumbach, Nancy Kruh, Karen Reiter, Diana Stewart, and Christine Wicker, my husband and helpmate, Tom, and my lovely in-laws, Tom and Jo Ann Battles. Everyone in the world should have friends and family as kind and generous.

Thanks to Laurie Helgoe, PhD, whose book *Introvert Power* crossed my desk and changed my life. And finally, thanks to the hundreds of introverts I have heard from over the years, whose comments on *The Introvert's Corner* blog have been encouraging, entertaining, and educational. In my first blog post, I urged introverts to unite—and we have. More power to us.

Index

acetylcholine, just settle down qualities of, 20

advantages of introversion, extrovert superiority called to question, 86–89

affirmations for introverts, spine stiffening qualities of, 176–79

Agreeableness (Big Five), 7, 58

alcohol
  party animal aspirations of hopeful introverts and, 109–12
  party animal aspirations of shy extroverts and, 15

aloneness vs. loneliness, lack of correlation between, 74–76

American culture, big stinkin' racket and introversion, 10–13

angry introverts
  and need to get over it, 183–84
  and pressure release, 22–24
  stupid stuff people say and, 154–56

antisocial misanthrope stereotype
  author's insecurity and, 1
  churlish introverts and, 36
  Eysenck's responsibility for, 7
  insulting extroverts and, 18
  misanthropic extroverts, 62
  and not taking it anymore, 24
  possible narcissism and, 85

arguments, and introvert/extrovert ground rules, 152

Aron, Elaine
  and confusing the definition of introversion, 9
  and HSP cottage industry, 18–19
  and living between dreams and reality, 33
  and sensory sensitivity theory, 8
  and theory of introvert overthinking, 26
  and why she might be right, 30

art galleries as fun, 125

asking questions party tactic and winding up an extrovert, 98–99

Asperger's syndrome, not necessarily, 145

athletics
  nice and quiet, 123
  not proof of extroversion, 2
  still not proof of extroversion, 31

audience participation as cruel and inhuman punishment, 120–21

babbling, the dreaded, 173–74

bathroom party tactic
  and adaptability to the office, 160
  to escape chatterboxes, 57
  to flee palaver, 98
  and multitasking, 94
  to prevent chitchat-related head explosion, 102

bathroom party tactic (*cont.*)
  to prolong party, 70
  sweet, sweet relief of, 93
  and yet more chatterboxes, 99
Big Five factors of personality
  and how crappy measurements of them
    can be, 58
  and how crappy the theory makes
    introversion seem, 7–8
birding festival, as experimental ground
    for my new approach to introversion,
    49–50
bitchy behavior (energy management)
  and doing other people a favor, 178
  and how it happens, 52–54
  and individual thresholds, 70–71
  and magic words to prevent, 55
  and training other people, 72
blogging
  as astonishing derring-do, 162
  authors propensity for, 132
  suitability for introverts of, 130
  and wise advice, 113–14
body language, using to not look bitchy
    and unapproachable, 37
"bombastic introvert," as describing
    Picasso, 162
bookshelves party tactic, as an excuse to
    turn your back, 93–94
boring people
  lack of responsibility for their happiness,
    100–103
  reminding yourself of that, 177–78
bottle, extroversion in a
  college party animal phase and, 15
  as a good way to annoy even yourself,
    109–12
boundaries
  and just quietly eating your dinner,
    56–57
  and not doing everything you partner
    wants, 151
brains of extroverts
  and Eysenck's guess, 7
  and faces, 18
  inability of introverts to put themselves
    into, 118
  and need for hubbub, 19–20
  and phone-related dopamine release,
    65–66
  whiz-bang technology and, 8
brains of introverts
  business of, 30

  and Eysenck's guess, 7
  horror of the telephone, 65–66
  possible reasons for party-induced
    catatonia, 18–21
  sleeping as a facsimile of, 42
  whiz-bang technology and, 8
Brando, Marlon, and effectiveness of
    mumbling, 12–13
breaks in workplace, taking, as cubicle
    survival tactic, 160
brotherhood and other kumbaya attitudes,
    183–85
Buddhists, author's inability to improve on
    the teachings of, 171
Buffett, Warren, as proof that extroverts
    don't necessarily rule, 88
bullying of introverts, Kristen
    Stewart as spokesperson against,
    154–56
business party tactic, all-purpose party-
    survival tactics useful for, 94–95

Canadian children study and acceptability
    of introversion, 87
Candid Camera (TV show), sheer horror
    of, 121
Carson, Johnny, as proof that introverts can
    sparkle, 162
cell phones, people yammering into, 101
charismatic leaders as attention hogs, 161
chatter vs. substantive conversation
  and astonishing quantities of words,
    100–101
  and happiness, 26–27
Cheek, Jonathan, shyness research of,
    82–83
Cheek and Buss scale for measurement of
    shyness, 83
children (parenting), relaxing with
    introversion of, 143–47
China
  popularity of quiet children in, 86–87
  increasing pissed-offness in, 185
chitchat, life-force-sucking qualities, 96–99
CMC (computer-mediated
    communication), not portending the
    end of civilization, 130–34
cocktail-party hell
  dullness of, 23
  necessity of chitchat in, 96–99
coffee shops, restorative qualities of, 124
"come out of our shell" and complete
    bullpoop of others' insistence, 4

computer-mediated communication
(CMC), not portending the end of
civilization, 130–34
conferences, tactics to make less
excruciating, 159
"Confessions of an Introverted Traveler"
(Dembling), as beginning of an
empire, 2
Conscientiousness (Big Five)
as another stable trait, 58
personality theory and, 7
conversation (substantive) vs. chatter
happiness and prattle, 26–27
startling quantities of words, 100–101
Copylicious (blog), excellent party-related
advice of, 113–14
costume parties, appalling lack of
inhibitions at, 121
Courage to Create, The (May), *dubious Rollo
May* quote from, 39
covert narcissism
sympathy for people suffering from,
82–83
and what it is not, 84
creativity and fertile void, introverts
relationship to, 39–43
Csikszentmihalyi, Mihaly, influential
concept of, 40
cubicle dwellers, misery of, 160

declining invitations
and defying FOMO, 106
to ensure they stop coming, 95
in order to enjoy parties, 182
as a legitimate prerogative, 177
and making up excuses, 107
and no good reason to go, 71–72
and not your problem, 56
saving psychic energy and, 49
and too damn tired, 64
deep processing
and brain overdrive, 19
as precursor to pretty much everything
we say and do, 41
deep thinkers
and being steamrolled in conversation, 31
lousiness at speed-oriented computer
games of, 29–30
default-mode network (DMN), as a racket
in introverts' minds, 169
definition of extroversion
according to personality theory, general
confusion, 7–8

according to theory and objectionable
stereotypes, 5–9
Freud's, Jung's, and Eysenck's, 6–7
in relation to introversion, 9
Dembling, Sophia, "Confessions of
an Introverted Traveler" and how this
whole introvert career got started, 2–3
Depp, Johnny, as introverted movie star, 12
depression
and extroverts' lack of, 86
and introverts' tendency toward, 87
*Diagnostic and Statistical Manual of Mental
Disorders* (DSM-5), introverts' umbrage
at possibly being included in, 20
Diana, Princess of Wales, bizarre
overwrought display of public grief at
the death of, 10–11
dinner parties
pleasantness of small, 92
unnecessary clown nose wearing at, 56–57
with wine and conversation, 124
DMN (default-mode network), introverts'
busy, 169
dog and pony show
behind the curtain of, 129
not a, 50
not proof of author's extroversion, 162
is optional, 178
putting on the extrovert is, 16
time to shut down the, 133
dopamine
extroverts' need for vs. introverts'
overwhelm from, 19–20
phone-precipitated rush of, 65–66
drawing as introvert fun, 125
drinking alcohol
as party tactic for shy extroverts, 15
as a bad idea, 109–12
DSM-5 *(Diagnostic and Statistical Manual
of Mental Disorders)* and pissed-off
introverts, 20
Dunbar, Robin, and anthropological
hocus-pocus, 126–27

email
as an alternative to the dreaded
telephone, 67
author's love affair with, 130–31
for career furtherance, 158–59
similarity to conversation, 132
unacceptable for all friendly contact, 180
energy drains, managing, to avoid
bitchiness, 55–57

energy in/energy out (psychic energy)
  according to Jung, 6
  and busy, busy introvert brains, 169–70
  and the mighty power of introversion, 78
  sounds good but who knows, 48–51
energy management (bitchy behavior)
  because we care, 72
  the most important skill of all, 52–54
  not wasting, as a favor to others, 178
  nuances of, 70–71
  and ugly introvert stereotypes, 55
enthusiasm and not dancing into room,
  79–80
escape hatch for parties as necessary skills,
  113–15
excuses (lying) as party escape hatch, 107
Expressiveness (IPIP-HEXACO)
  as an allegedly extroverted quality, 58
  lame measurement of, 59
Extroversion (Big Five)
  lame measurement of, 58
  words describing, 7
extroversion vs. introversion, 2, 3, 4
  advantages, 86–89
  alcohol, 15, 109–12
  American culture and, 11, 12
  angry introverts, 22–23, 24
  bitchy behavior, 52
  brains of extroverts, 7, 8, 18, 19–20,
    65–66, 118
  brotherhood, 183–85
  children (parenting), 143, 146
  definition of, 6–7, 7–8, 9
  energy drains, managing, 56
  energy in/energy out (psychic energy),
    48, 50, 51
  failed extroverts, introverts as, 58–61
  fertile void and creativity, 39–40, 41
  friendships, 127–28, 136–37, 138, 165
  fun, 119–22, 123
  happiness bias, 77, 78
  intensity of introverts, 25
  internal flame of introverts, 35, 36, 37
  introversion and, 135–38
  life through extrovert eyes, 116, 117–18
  love and relationships, 148–49, 150, 152–53
  middle ground, 181
  mistakes introverts make, 175
  narcissism, 84, 85
  "no" vs. "yes" to invitations, 104
  online extrovert, 130–34
  parties and, 71, 78, 79, 80–81, 90, 97, 98,
    99, 114, 115
  people, just not all the time, 62, 63
  shyness vs. introversion, 14, 15, 16, 17
  sitting and watching, 45, 46
  state vs. trait of extroversion, 77
  team-building, 157, 158, 159, 161
  telephones and introverts, 66
  thinking of introverts and, 30, 31, 33
Eysenck, Hans
  calls introverts phlegmatic, 30
  contribution to definition/misanthrope
    stereotype, 6–7
  introverts are a little bit, 9

Facebook
  "friends" vs. friends and the proper
    number thereof, 127
  as a godsend, 130
  good qualities of, 131
  irritating racket of, 133
  as an outlet for judgmental
    statements, 116
  public grief and tearstained pages of, 11
face-to-face interaction, unthreatened by
  online social networking, 131–32
false memories, or maybe it's creativity, 87
family issues
  tactics for dealing with, 139–42
  and why you know better, 179
fear of missing out (FOMO), when to
  ignore/respect, 106
fear vs. introversion, confusion
  between, 174
feats of derring-do
  dog and pony show and other, 162–63
  long, tedious stories about, 102
fertile void and creativity, accessible but
  not exclusive to introverts, 39–43
fifty ways to leave a party without pooping
  it, 113–15
fighting for right not to party
  and being accused of unpleasant things,
    70–73
  and "phone a friend" tactic, 95
f#&$ing hate it when you say that (angry
  introverts)
  and the f#&$ing hated stuff said, 154–56
  and pressure release, 22–24
  but stop the hating, 183–84
flâneur and liking to watch, 44–46
Fleeson, Will
  and his extrovert-centric research, 77–80
  and introvert power, 60–61
"flow" concept, introverts and, 40–41

FOMO (fear of missing out), genuine
missing out vs. imaginary, 106
franchise restaurants study and introverted
leaders, 161
Freud, Sigmund
accuses introverts of narcissism, 82
sex-obsessed Debbie Downer, 5
surly, 8
friendships
advantages of introversion, 87–88
extroversion and introversion, 127–28,
136–37, 138, 165
fun, 124
life through introvert eyes, 117
loneliness, 75
middle ground, 182
mistakes introverts make, 174–75
parties and introverts, 126
tips for making, 164–67
various levels of, 126–29
See also introversion
fun
accusations of not having, 3–4
not fun, 119–22
yes fun, 123-25

Gilot, Françoise, does and describes
Picasso, 162
goal setting for better living, 176–77
"going solo" vs. lousy date, etc., 76
Godfather, The (movie) and mumbling,
12–13
grief, public, orgy of, 10–11
Grimes, Jennifer
theory about energy investment, 50, 51
theory of getting stuff done, 41

happiness bias
happiness not one-size-fits-all, 104
Mountain Dew vs. International
Coffee, 123
yeah, maybe not, 77–81
Harrison, George, was a hound dog, 40
Harvard gives introverted leaders their
due, 88
Hax, Carolyn
advising an extrovert on boyfriends, 148
advising an introvert on
boyfriends, 137
headsets for phones as way to make the
telephone less onerous, 68
Helgoe, Laurie, and sitting and watching,
44–45

hell is a cocktail party
chitchat incubators, 96–99
and tyranny of extroverts, 23
Hepburn, Katharine, famously
introverted, 162
hermits
not an insult, 149
when to stop being, 107–8
Highly Sensitive Person (HSP)
jumbled into introversion definition, 8
jury is out on, 9
maybe it's introversion, 30
peering into the brain of, 18–19
holidays, the most difficult season, 140
HSP (Highly Sensitive Person)
as maybe not part of introversion
definition, 9
as part of introversion definition, 8
still not sure, 30
what the brain tells us, 18–19

imagination, author's infatuation with her
own, 33
impassive faces
appearance of dullness, 32
off-putting-ness of, 25
insta-friendships, not so easy anymore, 167
intensity of introverts
exhausting extroverts, 51
told we're too intense, 3
too much or just right, 25–28
interaction and serendipity in innovation, 41
internal flame of introverts, brightness,
heat, kindling and extinguishing, 32–34
Internet
godsend for introverts, 130
for ignoring annoying people, 131
for rekindling friendships, 165
introversion, 1–4
advantages of introversion, 86–89
affirmations for introverts, 176–79
alcohol, 15, 109–12
American culture and, 10–13
angry introverts, 22–24, 154–56, 183–84
bitchy behavior (energy management),
52–54, 55, 70–71, 72, 178
boring people, 100–103, 177–78
brains of introverts, 7, 8, 18–21, 30, 42,
65–66
brotherhood, 183–85
bullying of introverts, 154–56
children (parenting), 143–47
definition of, 5–9

introversion (*cont.*)
   energy drains, managing, 55–57
   energy in/energy out (psychic energy),
     6, 48–51, 78, 169–70
   extroversion and, 135–38
   extroversion vs., 2, 3, 4
   extroverts (failed), introverts as, 58–61
   family issues, 139–42, 179
   fear vs., 174
   feats of derring-do, 102, 162–63
   fertile void and creativity, 39–43
   fun, 3–4, 119–25
   happiness bias, 77–81, 104, 123
   intensity of introverts, 3, 25–28, 51
   internal flame of introverts, 32–34
   life through introvert eyes, 116–18
   listening by introverts, 100, 101–2, 103
   loneliness, 74–76, 126
   love and relationships, 148–53, 179
   middle ground, 180–82
   mind fullness to mindfulness, 168–71
   mistakes introverts make, 172–75
   narcissism, 82–85
   noise threshold of introverts, 10, 18, 30,
     38, 49, 62, 135–38, 169
   "no" vs. "yes" to invitations, 104–8, 177
   online extroverts, 130–34
   people, just not all the time, 62–64
   quietness, 13, 35–38
   shyness vs., 8–9, 14–17, 82, 83, 110–11, 163
   sitting and watching, 11, 44–47, 111
   team of one, 157–61
   telephones, 65–69, 151, 158–59, 173,
     178–79, 180–81
   thinking of introverts, 29–31
   See also extroversion vs. introversion;
     friendships; parties and introverts
Introvert Power (Helgoe) and being a
   flâneur, 45
"Introvert's Guide to Spontaneous
   Departures, An" (Parkinson), good
   advice in, 113–14
IPIP-HEXACO extroversion measuring
   tool, nitpicking of, 58–59
isolation, not so good for you, 172–73

Jackson, Michael, public grief and, 11
James, William, theory of emotion and
   behavior, 81
Japanese study and permission to latch
   on, 165
jigsaw puzzles as escapism during family
   togetherness, 141

Jobs, Steve, as yang, 89
Johns, Jasper, and dreaming, 42
judging, don't, 175
Jung, C. G.
   and deep thinking, 29
   flattering us, 32
   and ignoring theory of psychic
     energy, 78
   a little bit of, 9
   and that whole energy thing, 6
   and theory of psychic energy, 48

karaoke
   amazingly, some introverts like, 70
   and museum people, 122
   no thank you, 120
knitting
   as escape from family togetherness, 141
   as fun, 125

Laney, Marti
   makes us feel good, 9
   theories and pro-introvert
     movement, 8
leadership
   introvert vs. extrovert style, 88–89
   and questionable superiority of
     charisma, 161
learn-and-adjust for middle ground, not
   pissing friends off, 181
leaving a party because you want to,
   113–15
life satisfaction as part of happiness
   (conveniently ignored), 80
life through introvert eyes, differences
   from through extrovert eyes, 116–18
Likert-type scale and extrovert
   enthusiasm, 80–81
listening by introverts
   and bores, 100
   exhausting aspects of, 101–2
   and retreating to happy place in head,
     103
Liveliness (IPIP-HEXACO)
   cockamamie measurement of, 60
   measuring, 58
loneliness
   confused with alone, 74–76
   in a crowd, 126
love and relationships
   across the introvert/extrovert divide,
     148–53
   and boundaries, 179

lunching with a good friend as introvert fun, 124
lying (excuses), usefulness of fake diarrhea, 107

macro view, overlooked cogs in, 11–12
magic words to plug energy drains re: responsibilities and problems, 55–57
magnetic resonance imaging and highly sensitive people, 9
management of energy (bitchy behavior)
  to do everyone a favor, 178
  explaining, 72
  to help us leave the house, 70–71
  as a key skill for introverts, 52–54
  so as not to get sucked into others' demands, 55
managing energy drains, magic words for, 55–57
Mardi Gras party and wearing beads, 114
marriages (introverts and extroverts)
  affirmation to help, 179
  negotiating for happy, 148–53
Martin, Steve
  famous introvert, 88
  public clown, 162
May, Rollo, on creativity, 39
McCartney, Paul, dreaming up "Yesterday," 42
McMaster University, research out of, 14
McMillan, Donna, uncovers extroverts' need to crank it up to, 11, 80–81
memory
  extroverts allegedly have better, 86
  or maybe introverts are more creative, 87
middle ground, finding, to keep friends, 180–82
mind fullness to mindfulness, not so easy, 168–71
mining your past to dig up friends, 165–66
misanthrope stereotype
  author tries on, 1
  and churlish introverts, 36
  Eysenck's culpability for, 7
  just saying no to, 24
  introverts' culpability for, 18
  and not being anti-people, 62
  relationship to narcissism, 85
mistakes introverts make, owning up to, 172–75
mixed marriages (introverts and extroverts)
  challenges and solutions, 148–53
  holding your own in, 179

monologue conversations, tedium of, 100
Mountain Dew
  how commercials define "fun," 123
  wrestling "fun" back from, 125
movies
  loud and dull, 34
  pleasure of sitting in the dark during, 124
  who cares about writers of, 12
Mozart, confusing place on the introvert/ extrovert continuum of, 39–40
museums
  as couples' compromise, 151
  and dead people, 121–22
  as inner flame fanners, 33
  as introvert fun, 125

narcissism and what we're not, 82–85
nascent friendships, weighing value of, 128
networking events, necessity of small talk at, 98
Neuroticism (Big Five)
  in personality theory, 7
  as a stable trait, 58
neurotransmitters
  dopamine vs. acetylcholine, 19–20
  phone-triggered, 65–66
never-met-a-stranger people
  author definitely is not one of those, 164
  lovely but exhausting friend of the author, 182
  nothing to do with loneliness, 75
  as one facet of extroversion, 2
Nielsen
  finds more texting than talking, 69
  reiterating this, 131
Nobel Prize, resulting from a dream, 42
noise threshold of introverts
  America exceeds, 10
  and conversations, 62
  and extroverts and happy noise, 135–38
  in our own brains, 169
  lowers when energy is depleted, 49
  and the need for quiet corners, 38
  and sensory sensitivity, 30
  similar to HSPs, 18
"noisy" shows and the American way, 10
"no" vs. "yes" to invitations
  spine-stiffening affirmations for, 177
  and weighing the decision, 104–8

office parties and the dreaded small talk, 98
online extroverts are also online introverts, 130–34

Openness (Big Five)
  and personality theory, 7
  as a stable trait, 58
Oprah (TV show) and Kristen Stewart's
  offensive reticence, 154
overt narcissism
  leaves trail of tears, 83
  vs. covert, 82
  why you're not (perhaps), 84

pain threshold of introverts related to
  sensory sensitivity, 30
painting
  and introvert passion, 79
  is mostly solitary (artist/model hanky-
    panky notwithstanding), 42
  as quiet success, 11
parenting and need to love little introverts,
  143–47
Parkinson, Kelly
  excellent party-exit advice from, 113–14
  and new and shiny friend, 115
parks, sitting quietly in, 125
parties and introverts
  alcohol, 15, 109–12
  American culture and, 13
  bathroom tactic, 57, 70, 93, 94, 95, 98, 99,
    102, 160
  boring people, 102–3
  brains of introverts, 19
  bullying of introverts, 156
  children, 146
  cocktail-party hell, 23, 96–99
  declining invitations, 49, 56, 64, 71–72,
    95, 106, 107, 177, 182
  energy drains, managing, 56–57
  energy in/energy out, 51
  escape hatch for parties, 113–15
  extroversion and, 71, 78, 79, 80–81, 90, 97,
    98, 99, 114, 115
  feats of derring-do, 163
  fighting for right not to party, 70–73, 95
  friendships, 126
  life through introvert eyes, 118
  love and relationships, 151
  mind fullness to mindfulness, 170
  mistakes introverts make, 173
  "no" vs. "yes" to invitations, 104–8, 177
  online extroverts, 131, 133
  pooping a party, 156
  predicament of parties, 90–92
  sensitivity to outside stimuli and, 8
  shyness vs. introversion, 15

sitting and watching, 11, 46
survival skills for parties, 93–95
See also introversion
passion, don't even suggest introverts
  lack, 79
past, mining your, as source of new old
  friends, 165–66
"Pathological Introversion," if they
  must, 20
people, just not all the time, liking of, 62–64
personality psychology
  measurement tool of, 58
  relation to introversion of, 7–8
Petrilli, Lisa, advice about conferences, 159
pets party tactic, chatting up of, 94
phlegmatic, in Eysenck's description of
  introverts, 30
"phone-a-friend" party tactic as not
  a lie, 95
phones and introverts
  and extroverts, 151
  and loathing, 65–69
  making a bad impression, 158–59
  and nonmandated response, 178–79
  and not messing up friendships, 180–81
  picking it up sometimes, 173
photography as party tactic, success in
  using, 94
physiological basis of introversion, we like
  the idea of, 7
Picasso, Pablo, paramour's description
  of, 162
planting yourself in a spot party tactic
  can backfire, 102–3
  and waiting for minglers, 95
plunging into the deep end, off-putting at
  the onion dip, 173
politics, bellowing qualities of, 11
pooping a party, hate being
  accused of, 156
positive affect
  extrovert-centric description of, 79
  as a one-legged stool, 80
practical jokes, horror of, 121
predicament of parties, whether or not to
  go, 90–92
problems and people's expectations, to hell
  with them, 56–57
professional success
  alleged extrovert superiority, 86
  Warren Buffet and, 88
"pro-introvert" movement, Marti Laney's
  early voice in, 8

psychic energy (energy in/energy out)
  busy minds as, 169–70
  Jung and, 6
  management of, whatever it is, 48–51
  not part of happiness research, 78
public speaking, no biggie, 163
Punk'd (TV show), author's aversion to, 121

question asking party tactic for less tedious
    chitchat, 98–99
quietness
  controlling the messages behind, 35–38
  introverts speaking out with, 13

reading, yes, please, 124
reality shows, salaries vs. librarian
    salaries, 12
Reeves, Nancy, calling introverts self-
    righteous, 33
relationships and love
  irrelevance of good intentions in, 179
  working out of, 148–53
responsibility and people's expectations,
    not so much, 56–57
restaurants, extrovert judgment of couple
    in, 116–17
road trips
  author's creativity during, 41–42
  pleasure of even repetitive, 124–25
Roberts, Julia
  in extrovert mode, 12
  identifies as introvert, 162
rumination as good way to feel bad, 26

Sartre, Jean-Paul, misquoted, 75
savasana and the busy mind, 169
Schmidt, Louis A., research of, 14–15
"self-righteous" introverts, attitude that
    earns the description of, 33
sensitivity to outside stimuli and parties
    and author's party-induced catatonia, 8
sensory processing
  and brains on overdrive, 30
  and feasting on the world, 45
  and introverts vs. HSPs, 8
sewing, introvert fun, 125
shyness vs. introversion
  and boozing it up, 110–11
  discussed more or less scientifically, 14–17
  mistakenly equated, 8–9
  and mother's accusation of narcissism, 82
  and overt vs. covert narcissism, 83
  and people's confusion, 163

sitting and watching
  as a flâneur, 44–47
  and happy hubbub, 11
  and witnessing cautionary behavior, 111
skinny-dipping as not-fun, 121
Skype as telephone alternative, 181
sleeping and creativity as an argument for
    introvert creativity, 42
sleeping in while not actually
    sleeping, 125
small talk, torture and necessity of, 96–99
smiling faces
  and looking intimidating, 27
  opacity of, 25
smoking party tactic
  author's nostalgia for, 94
  and smoking vicariously, 112
sociability
  Eysenck and, 6–7
  and introverts' needs, 36
  and introvert's selectiveness, 63–64
  and introverts' social skills, 16
  motivation towards, 14
  and unhappiness of shy extroverts, 15
Sociability (IPIP-HEXACO)
  crummy definition of, 59–60
  measurement of, 58
Social Boldness (IPIP-HEXACO)
  measurement of, 58
  offensive definition of, 59
"Social Withdrawal" as in the DSM, 20
solitude
  discerning need for, 104
  good things that happen in, 42
  negotiating time for, 152
  pleasant implications of, 75–76
spectating
  as a flâneur, 44–47, 111
  instead of doing the conga, 11
"spiritual fun," not an oxymoron, 125
Spirituality for Extroverts (Reeves),
    accusatory reference, 33
sports
  extroverts as good (i.e., always game),
    135
  introvert vs. extrovert, 31
  introvert-friendly, 123
  not part of extroversion definition, 2
spot (planting yourself in) party tactic
  as author's favorite, 95
  risks of, 102–3
state vs. trait of extroversion, definition
    of, 77

stay-put party tactic
    danger of, 102–3
    spongelike quality of, 95
Stelmack, Robert
    smacks down author;s theory, 30
    theory about extrovert athletes, 31
Stewart, Kristen
    going all, 156
    f#&$ing hates it when they say that,
        154–55
stress
    extroverts allegedly suffer less, 86
    and introverts being goaded to
        change, 87
substantive conversation vs. chatter
    and boring introverts into a stupor,
        100–101
    research into, 26–27
superficial relationships, pros and cons of,
    127–28
supermarket duty as escape, 141
"surrogates," acceptable for shy people,
    165
survival skills for parties, arsenal of, 93–95
swimming, delightfully solitary nature
    of, 124

team of one and extroverts at work, 157–61
telephones
    compromising with friends over, 180–81
    ignoring of, 178–79
    and pissing off friends, 173
    and professional failure, 158–59
    and relationship tension, 151
    as tool of the devil, 65–69
texting
    as CMC, 130
    etiquette of new friendships and, 166
    and mobile phones, 131
    mobile phones used more often for, 69
    as primary tool of communication, 67
theaters, appeal of sitting in the dark
    in, 124
thinking of introverts, deep and slow, 29–31
thought, translating to speech, and lag time
    for introverts, 30–31
tips for making friends, leaving the house
    and other, 164–67
trait vs. state of extroversion, explanation
    of, 77

Tumblr, introvert facility for, 132
TV
    gorging on, 125
    noisy shows on, 10
    reality shows on, 12
Twilight (movies), pissed-off star of, 154
Twitter and introvert style, 133

UCLA Loneliness Scale, not measuring
    number of friends, 75
USA Today, article about leadership in, 88

vacations as introvert/extrovert stress
    point, 150–51

Wake Forest University, annoying study
    out of, 77
walking
    as escape from excessive togetherness,
        140–41
    introverts' enjoyment of, 124
watching, sitting and
    and being a flâneur, 44–47
    rather than adding to the racket, 11
    witnessing sloppy behavior while, 111
weddings
    and hellish chitchat, 98
    manning up for, 90
    precipitating nightmare moment for
        author, 91
World Hum website, launching author's
    introversion career, 2
Wozniak, Steve, as yin, 89
writing
    to argue, 152
    as derring-do, 162
    done in a quiet room, 42
    and ghostwriting, 12
    home preferable to cubicle for, 160
    as introvert fun, 125
    pithy memos at work, 158
    as a preferred means of communication,
        130
    as quiet success, 11

"Yesterday" (McCartney), dreamed up, 42
"yes" vs. "no" to invitations
    making decisions regarding, 104–8
    as one small step, 177
yoga and author's failure at savasana, 169